Illinois Central College
Learning Resource Center

E G L'I

GREATNESS IN LITERATURE

AND OTHER PAPERS

BY

W. P. TRENT *1862 - 1939*

PROFESSOR OF ENGLISH LITERATURE IN COLUMBIA UNIVERSITY

Essay Index Reprint Series

BOOKS FOR LIBRARIES PRESS, INC.

FREEPORT, NEW YORK

PN
58
.T7
1967

First published 1905
Reprinted 1967

LIBRARY OF CONGRESS CATALOG CARD NUMBER:

67-26790

PRINTED IN THE UNITED STATES OF AMERICA

PREFACE

THIS volume might have been described as a collection of literary addresses rather than of "papers," since far the larger portion of its contents was prepared for delivery on academic occasions. Everything, however, has been somewhat altered for publication, whether here or in the magazines from which I have been kindly allowed to reprint some articles; hence I have adopted the rather non-committal term "papers." I could not bring myself to employ that delightful and alluring word "essays," because that connotes to my mind a discursive charm which, perhaps, I could not impart to any composition, and which I certainly did not try to impart to most of the writings here collected. In every case except the last paper I was pursuing, successfully or unsuccessfully, a line of thought rather than loitering in the highways and byways of appreciative criticism. This fact, or what I think to be a fact, seemed at least not obscured by the

use of the term "papers," whereas, if I had
employed the term "essays," I should have run
the risk of beguiling some readers not acquainted
with my idiosyncratic deficiencies into suppos-
ing that they were taking up a book designed
primarily to give them pleasure. I should be
delighted to give pleasure, and I sincerely hope
I shall give no pain; but my main object is to
discuss certain topics with all the readers I can
secure, especially with those who like myself are
interested in the problems that confront the critic
and the teacher of literature. But now, having
done my best to warn off any reader who is on
the lookout for true essays and to indicate the
class of persons likely, if any are, to find something to their account in my volume, I leave that
newcomer into the world of books to take care
of itself.

                                    W. P. TRENT.
NEW YORK,
    March 11, 1905.

CONTENTS

v

I

THE QUESTION OF
"GREATNESS IN LITERATURE"

[Prepared originally in answer to some queries propounded by students of a course given in the Columbia Summer Session of 1901. Delivered as a lecture in Cincinnati, December, 1901. Published in *The International Monthly* for May, 1902.]

THE QUESTION OF
"GREATNESS IN LITERATURE"

IT is hard to conceive of a rasher attempt, at least in the sphere of thought, than the one implied by the title above. A discussion of "greatness in literature," and of some of the standards by which it may be determined, involves the inference that the person who voluntarily enters upon it, thinks he knows something definite about a matter over which critics have been disputing for centuries as violently as physicians and theologians have wrangled over their respective topics of contention. Such an implication hampers both him who conducts a discussion and him who follows it. Yet it is obvious that if every man stood in awe of being deemed presumptuous, and kept silence with regard to all vexed problems, few attempts would be made either to settle or to come nearer settling them. In consequence, the world of thought would almost stand still and the world of action, to use a homely phrase, would surely slow down. A certain amount of rashness in

3

theorizing is therefore permissible, especially in connection with topics of marked importance, even though the results obtained should, after all, appear very commonplace.

That it is important to be able, approximately, to estimate "greatness in literature" seems apparent. Never before has literature meant so much to the public at large as it does in our democratic age, in which books are wonderfully cheap and education is widely diffused. It follows that the struggle between good books and bad, between great books and trivial, has never before meant so much to mankind. When readers were few, the harm done by bad or poor books was comparatively limited, and the world could often well afford to allow time to do the necessary sifting. But now that we are all readers, now that our daily newspapers describe countless new books and new editions, while our department stores set them before our eyes at any price we may have fixed upon, the question how we may best pick and choose among the thousands of volumes offered us, is one that many conscientious men and women who care for literature cannot dismiss lightly, despite the fact that there is no lack of genial eclectic lovers of books to tell them, with

more than a grain of truth, that overserious reading is one of the banes of our self-conscious age.
But this question of the Choice of Books, about
which critics like Frederic Harrison have written
helpfully and delightfully, is indissolubly involved
with the question of "greatness in literature,"
and of the standards by which this may be determined. The marked importance of the latter
question being thus apparent, the rashness of
discussing it is minimized, and further apologies
may be waived.

The use of the word "greatness" implies standards of comparison, which may be individual or
collective. It is clear that a poem or other piece
of literature may be great to me and not to the
rest of the world, or that it may be accepted as
great by a majority of critics and readers and not
seem at all great to me. Furthermore, a piece
of literature may be great to contemporaries of
its author and by no means great to posterity, or
vice versa, — although, as a matter of fact, it seldom happens that posterity sees real greatness in
what did not profoundly appeal to contemporaries.
It often sees interest, charm, but rarely greatness.

From these facts we infer that collective standards are not of paramount value when they

merely involve contemporary appreciation of a book or writer, but that they do gain very great value when they have been held by a number of generations. For example, it is probably not wise, but it is certainly permissible, to affirm that Tennyson is not a great poet. It would be the height of unwisdom to maintain that Homer is not a great poet, provided we admit his existence, or to announce as Joel Barlow, our own half-forgotten epic poet, once did, in a far from Platonic style, that Homer has exerted a most immoral influence on mankind. But while this is true, it is equally true that our individual standards are of paramount importance to us as individuals. If we cannot see that the "Iliad" is great, we are reduced to three unpleasant modes of procedure, — we either stifle our thoughts, or pretend to admire what we do not, which is unedifying conventionality or rank hypocrisy, or else as Herbert Spencer did in his "Autobiography," we proclaim our disagreement with the world's verdict, and run the risk of being sneered at or called stupid by people whose acquaintance with Homer is probably far from profound.

Such being the case, we may infer that it is a matter of some importance, if we care for litera-

ture at all, for us who study or read books, to put
our individual standards as far as possible in accord with the collective standards.   In this way we
shall approximate true culture; to apply Matthew
Arnold's words, we shall learn to know and agree
with the best that has been thought and said
in the world about literature.   This is not all of
culture, but it is a most important part of it.   It
is only fair to add, however, that a whole school
of critics has of late more or less denied the need
of our taking account of collective standards.
These are the Impressionists, well represented
by M. Jules Lemaître, and their shibboleth seems
to be, "I like this book; if you don't, you can keep
your own opinion and I'll keep mine."   This is a
very independent, and ostensibly liberal, statement
of principles, and it is naturally popular; but a fool
can make it as complacently as a wise man, and it
leads to chaos in matters of taste.   In its extreme
forms, impressionism is individualism run mad, and
has few or no uses; in more moderate forms it
has uses which, however, need not be discussed
here.

But what has all this to do with the question of
"greatness in literature"?   This much at least.
Greatness implying standards of comparison, those

standards being individual and collective, and the collective being the more important of the two, but the individual nearer to us, it seems to follow that we ought first to examine our own ideas of "greatness in literature," then consult the chief critics to determine what writings the collective wisdom of mankind has pronounced great, and finally try to corroborate and enlarge our own ideas by means of such consultation and of wide reading. In this process we start with what is nearest to us, our own feelings and thoughts, and widen out our conceptions until we embrace as much of the universal as we can. This appears to be logical and to be analogous with other mental processes.

Now how do we as individuals use the term "great" in connection with literature? We use it loosely, but no more loosely than in other connections, and presumably we use it mainly of things or persons that do something, not of things or persons that are on the whole quiescent, no matter how full they may be of potential energy. The great statesman, for example, is to each of us the man who accomplishes something in the sphere of politics, not the man who has merely the potentialities of success. And he must accomplish something which in our view is large, important, influential, com-

paratively permanent, more or less original, and
unique, or we shall not call him great — at least
we shall not call him great for long. Do we not
apply the term with respect to literature in some
such way? The poem or the poet, the book or
the writer, must do something with us, and
that something must be large, important, influential, comparatively permanent, more or less
original, and unique. Obviously there are two
spheres in which this large, important something
may be done, — the sphere of our emotions and
the sphere of our intelligence. One book stirs
our feelings deeply and permanently; another
opens out a range of new ideas which make an
impression upon our lives; we call both these
books great, and rightly.

Perhaps I may venture by way of illustration
to give two instances out of my own experience.
When I first read it, I called Balzac's "Père
Goriot" a great book because the life of the
devoted old father who gave up everything for
his heartless daughters, left upon me a large
and deep impression of the power of the pater-
nal instinct; it left a permanent sense of the
pathos of much of this mortal life; it was important and influential, I trust, in widening my

sympathies; and the novel seemed original and unique because I saw that Balzac had not imitated Shakspere in "Lear," but had accomplished the wonderful feat of taking a situation not dissimilar to that treated by Shakspere, and developing it into something very different from "Lear," and almost as impressive, though not so grandly poetical. So I called that a great novel when I first read it, and I have continued to call it such.[1] The other book I shall mention only, but its effects upon me might be analyzed as easily. It was Gibbon's "Decline and Fall of the Roman Empire." That book enlarged my knowledge and my conception of history so immensely and permanently that I rose from perusing its final pages as certain of its tremendous greatness as I was of my own existence. But it should be observed that while Gibbon's great history affects the mind primarily, it affects the emotions also, — think of the splendid pictures it contains, — and that

[1] Whether I or any one else should call Turgenev's "Lear of the Steppes" great or merely impressive is a point that may be raised in this connection, but not discussed here. The universality of the appeal made by the Lear story is curiously illustrated by the fact that it has been recently made the motive of a Yiddish play by Mr. Jacob Gordin.

"Père Goriot," while it affects the emotions primarily, affects the mind also by giving it many fresh ideas about human, and especially French, life. It follows that while it is convenient to distinguish between the two spheres in which literature acts, — the emotions and the intelligence, — as a matter of fact, almost every piece of good literature will operate in both. One cannot really separate, for purposes of isolation, the effects of a book any more than one can so separate, save in theory, the faculties of the person that feels those effects.

From these two instances of the application of the individual standard to determine "greatness in literature," let us turn to consider the application of the collective standards. With regard to "Père Goriot" and the "Decline and Fall" I knew long beforehand that the world had pronounced them both to be great books. It was, therefore, not necessary to verify my main conclusions, although I have found it worth while to read criticisms of Balzac and Gibbon in order to determine, if I could, whether the various grounds on which I based my judgments were correctly taken. That is usually a very good thing to do. But it may easily happen, especially if we are not widely read, or are desultory in our reading, that we may chance upon a book the name and reputation of which are unfamiliar to us, which nevertheless moves us profoundly and seems to us great. This is a case for using the collective standards. We may find that the book has for years been regarded as great by a sufficient number of readers fairly to entitle it to rank as a classic, — in which case our own standards are proved to be in harmony with those of the world, and we are encouraged more and more to trust to our own judgments. This is the way, it seems to me, that we best educate ourselves in literature, — by constantly reading and verifying the judgments we pass, — not slavishly, not giving up our own points of view simply because we do not find the best critics on our side, and, on the other hand, not dogmatically or egotistically maintaining our own views, — but quietly and with an open mind confirming our presumably correct judgments, and reconsidering and revising our presumably erroneous ones by reading and conversation and reflection.

But in case the book we have accidentally read and thought great is condemned by the critics, or not even mentioned by them, what are we to conclude? That we were entirely mistaken? That is scarcely necessary. The book has done great things for us, and is truly great thus far. We may be the one reader out of a thousand for whom the author was writing, — his fit audience, though very few. It may be because the book or poem suited a transient mood. It may be because it suited our special epoch of life, or our class instincts and prepossessions, or what not. Here we have a reason why books are immensely popular with one generation, yet are scarcely read by the next. Generations change, — progressing in some ways, losing in others, but, as we trust, on the whole progressing. What wonder, then, that the book which exactly suited our fathers, but did not go much below the surface, so as to touch permanent ideas and emotions uniquely and profoundly should be unread to-day! As we rise in culture, we leave behind a novelist like E. P. Roe, and turn to Thackeray; but this does not mean that we should sneer at the popular American novelist, or at the people who liked his books, — much less at those who still like them, — any more than it means that on first reading "Henry Esmond" and finding it delightful, we should naïvely write a letter commending it to the readers of our favorite literary weekly.

Are we not led to conclude that there is a relative "greatness in literature," as well as, what we may call for convenience, an absolute greatness, and that we can safely use the word "great" only in connection with works that have stood the collective standards successfully? It seems better for practical purposes to emphasize the latter conclusion. Let us call that "great" which has produced large, important, influential, permanent, original, and unique results both in ourselves and in a majority of readers and critics, past and present. Let us insert a "perhaps" or a "probably" or some other qualification before the word "great" used of any living writer, except, it may be, in the case of an author like Count Tolstoy, whose chief works have been long before the world, and have attained that cosmopolitan fame which as a criterion of merit is no bad substitute for the fame awarded by time. This may seem cold and heartless and pedantic, yet it surely raises the dignity of literature, and gives us a better chance for free and honest contemporary criticism.

But let us look for a moment at the negative side of the question. If we so limit the word "great" in its application, what terms are we to apply to the enormous masses of literature that lie below the line of greatness? There are several terms that seem available. The writings that have appealed to us and to those similarly minded may be delightful, as in the case of the society poetry of Matthew Prior. They may be charming, as in the case of the delicate verses of Mr. Austin Dobson. They may be good, as in the case of perhaps eight out of ten of the poets who survive sufficiently to be represented at considerable length in such a standard anthology as Mr. Humphry Ward's "English Poets," or of the essayists and novelists whose works continue to be published in uniform collected editions. Probably at least eight-tenths of the literature which the best critics discuss ranges from fair to good as a whole. If it is only fair, we need not read it, unless we are trying to make critics of ourselves, or historians of literature; and we can tell very accurately whether it is only fair by observing the amount of attention it receives from critics whose judgments we have learned to respect. In the case of good literature, — a very considerable amount of which is being written to-day all over the world, — we must pick and choose. We should have to live to be a thousand years old to read it all or nearly all, and our real concern is with the great, and with that portion of the delightful, the charming, and the good that makes a special appeal to us as individuals. It is plain that we must discover for ourselves this specially appealing literature, for no one else has precisely our tastes; but we may, of course, be aided by wide reading in criticism, and by using the other instrumentalities of culture.

It goes without saying that there are other classes of books, or rather that the term "good literature" may be resolved into various classes. One book is interesting, because the main fact of which we are conscious when we put it down is that it held our attention remarkably well. We read on and on to see what the end would be. We did not pause for contemplation, we felt no rapture, — if we had, probably we should have pronounced it "great" immediately, — but we did feel interest, we recommended the book to our friends, and perhaps were among the hundred thousand readers whom the jubilant publisher advertised in every conspicuous place. Another book is valuable, because we frequently make use of it or of the ideas it contains. Another is agreeable, because it helps us to while away the time.

Against these books, when they have not through the lapse of years become standard, it would be only a pessimistic, almost an inhuman, critic who would inveigh; they have become necessaries of life. What would the publishers or the literary supplements of the newspapers do without them? But they are either not literature at all, or else in many cases lie outside the province of the serious critic or of the teacher and student of literature. That enigmatical personage, the average reader, is fully capable of attending to them without assistance.

There is, however, one further class of compositions that needs a word. There are books, and especially single poems, which it is our first impulse to call beautiful. Are these really great?

We may safely answer, "Yes," provided they are truly and more or less completely beautiful, and provided the beauty is pure and elemental. Keats's line will help us here, "A thing of beauty is a joy forever." An eternal joy is bound, unless there is something the matter with us, to produce in us large, permanent, important, and unique emotions. Thus it is that many of the poems of Keats himself are great poems in a true sense, — although they may seem at first thought to lie outside the sphere of our normal life, and thus to lack vitality. As their loveliness takes possession of us, it energizes our souls, perhaps just as much, in the case of many of us, as the more obvious power and passion and contagious optimism of Browning do. But if the work is merely beautiful in parts, not as a whole, — if it is the so-called purple passages that affect us, — then it is no more great than a picture of a woman is great, merely because the painter has succeeded in giving her a pair of beautiful eyes. And if we suspect that the poem or book is merely pretty, if it leaves us with a sense of placid contentment, we may be very sure that it is not great for us. Some of Longfellow's poetry appears, as we advance in culture, to produce fainter impressions upon us than it did upon our fathers and mothers, — which is perhaps the chief reason why we are hearing so many people assert that he is not a great poet. Personally, I think that some injustice is being done to Longfellow, but the main point here is to understand why with many readers his work seems to have lost ground.

Now, while Longfellow has apparently been losing ground, another American poet, Edgar Allan Poe, has been gaining it. This leads us naturally to consider a question fully as important as that of "greatness in literature," to wit, What standards must we apply in order to determine the relative greatness of writers? After we have learned approximately to recognize the best literature, we are almost inevitably bound to observe that, while we may call two books great, and refrain from further comparison, we cannot in most cases disguise the fact that we find one decidedly superior to the other, and that thus we pass to asking the question which author is the greater.

But some critics and readers, notably the Impressionists, object to this emphatically. Why not be content, they say, with the fact that you like this writer for one reason and that for another? Why run down any one? Why compare writers when it is almost certain that you do not know them equally well, and are thus in constant danger of being unfair? Why try to measure what is incommensurable, since you cannot measure so subtle a thing as literature, at least when it is imaginative, and you have no inflexible standards?

There is truth in this point of view so far as it involves a protest that we should not discriminate against one writer, because by our standards we find another greater. A catholic taste will enjoy everything that is good. Our love for Shakspere and Milton need not impair our affection for Charles Lamb and Goldsmith and Irving. Great writers will kill mediocre or bad writers ; for example, many people cannot read trashy novelists after the masters of fiction, — but no great author ever really injures by comparison a genuinely good one, who has done well his own work no matter how small. Thus we see from the world's experience that the attempt to rank men of letters has not annihilated or cast into the shade the lesser authors who have genuine qualities, and that the plea of the Impressionist against running writers down does not in fact apply to us when we set up our standards of measurement.

But there is a positive reason for setting up these standards, which the Impressionist is likely to overlook. It is a law of the human mind and heart to seek the best and to pay it due homage when found. Could we check the operations of this law, we should do much to stop human progress, much to sap the foundations of society. The law is universal; it is seen in monarchies and republics, in politics and literature; nay, more, is it not the main-spring of every religion? The highest deserves the utmost homage, when, in that highest, truth, beauty, and goodness are found in supreme measure. How useless, then, to ask us to stop applying our standards; that is, to stop measuring to determine the highest!

For generations on generations men have been comparing the various arts, and on the whole have given the palm to poetry, for reasons which may be found in such critics as Aristotle and Lessing. All the other arts have their advocates and lovers, of course; but thus far the consensus of opinion seems to be in favor of poetry, and for the present we can let the question stand as if it were settled, although, as a matter of fact, it is anything but settled. Then, by inexorable law, men began to classify poetry, and to ask which kind of poetry is greatest. Here, again, there is no unanimity of opinion; but collective standards, which in these more or less general and abstruse subjects are the only safe ones to use, have put either the poetic tragedy or the epic first, have placed the impassioned, highly wrought ode above all other forms of lyric, and have ranked the satire and the didactic poem beneath the other categories of poetry. This is not saying, to be sure, that a very good satire may not be better than a mediocre or even a fairly good ode, nor is it saying that the kinds of poetry are not frequently fused, not to say confused — the only point that need be emphasized here is that, since the days of the Greeks, there has been what may be called a *hierarchy of the literary species*,[1] — that is, a ranking of the kinds of literature, especially of poetry, — and that if we are to give this up, we must do so for better reasons than are advanced by the critics who will have none of it.

But just as there has been a comparison of the arts and of the kinds of literature, so there has been a comparison of the artists and the writers. The poets, for example, have been compared and ranked according to the kinds of poetry they have attempted, and according to the total power and value of their work. Thus, until Shakspere arose, Homer was regarded as not merely the Father of Poets, but as, take him all in all, the

---

[1] Perhaps the best equivalent we have for the French term *genre* when it is applied to literature. "Categories," which is sometimes employed in this connection, does not seem to be altogether satisfactory.

greatest of poets. Some of us still think him the greatest, but nearly all the world has given the palm to Shakspere. There is room, however, in this case as in others, for the individual standard to apply, because it is generally admitted by persons who know both poets that they are so very great that estimating their greatness is almost like taking the altitudes of two tremendous mountains of nearly equal heights. The slightest deflection of the instrument may cause an error; it is permissible, therefore, to take new measurements from time to time. So it is with Milton and Dante. But merely because two sets of observers differed slightly in their measurements of those two mountains, would be no reason whatever for inferring either that the mountains were not very high or that the methods employed in observing them were without scientific value. Just so, because there may be some question still whether Shakspere is greater than Homer, or *vice versa*, — we are assuming, to be sure, that Shakspere wrote his own plays and that the name "Homer" does not cover a multitude of singers, — is no reason for denying the proposition that they are in all probability the two most marvellously endowed poets that ever lived, or for holding that the collective standards applied to determine their unique greatness are valueless.

But enough has probably been said on these points; let us turn to the practical matter of endeavoring to determine how authors are to be ranked in the scale of greatness. One fact seems settled, — it is that there is a small group of what are sometimes called world-writers, — writers, chiefly poets, supremely great; who are read in nearly every land and in some cases have been so read almost since they wrote; who are separated in point of genius by a wide chasm from all other authors. The writers of universal genius we may call them, although supreme writers is, probably, a better designation. They are very few in number; Homer, Sophocles, Virgil, Dante, Shakspere, Milton, Goethe, nearly exhaust the list. Molière, however, should be added because he represents the comedy of manners so marvellously, and we should doubtless include Cervantes and a few others. It is clear that the authors named are supreme in their excellence, and it is also obvious that they have no living peers. In fact, there are scarcely more than three recent writers known to us who seem possibly entitled to such a high rank, and they are Scott, Victor Hugo, and Balzac, about whom the critics are still arguing *pro* and *con.*

Below these masters, yet far above the majority even of authors to whom the term "great" is freely applied, comes a small group of writers of very eminent originality and power, of great reputation outside their own nationalities, but still not universal in their genius, nor so dazzling in their achievements as the supreme or world writers. This group is often not separated from the classes above it and below it; hence there is no classification for it that is accepted everywhere. It will not do to apply Mr. Swinburne's suggestive division of poets as gods and giants, because, while it is fairly easy to recognize a giant, the gleaming presence of some divinities, especially of Mr. Swinburne's own, is occasionally hidden from mortal eyes. Then, again, there are semi-divinities; indeed, there is no telling how minutely the divine essence may be parcelled out. In the case of the men of letters we are now discussing it might be permissible to call them the *dii minores,* — the minor divinities of literature, if we chose to call the world-writers the *dii majores,* — the major divinities of literature; emphasis being laid on the fact that they differ from all authors below them in fairly seeming to surpass in their power and influence what merely great writers might be expected to accomplish. This implies, it is true, a somewhat stable standard of level greatness, a point which we shall discuss in a moment, and there is probably no need at this late day of taking refuge in such an undefinable term as "divinities." It is, perhaps, better to distinguish this class as that of the very great writers. Into it would seem to fall such poets as Pindar in Greek, Lucretius in Latin, Petrarch, Tasso, and Ariosto in Italian, Chaucer and Spenser in English, Schiller and Heine in German. It is not unlikely that some critics, desiring to give the French a place in the list, would insert the name of Victor Hugo; but, as we have just seen, he is a candidate for higher honors, and personally I should unhesitatingly assign those same higher honors to Voltaire for his excellence in prose and verse combined. But whatever we may say of French poets, there are at least two masters of French prose who seem very great, — Rabelais and Montaigne, — and to balance them we may name two very great British prose writers, Swift and Gibbon.

But we must be tentative in our illustrations, for there is little unanimity among the critics, as may be seen by comparing the rank given Chaucer by Matthew Arnold with that given him, let us say, by Professor Lounsbury. Not a few of us would doubtless like to assert emphatically the supreme position of the author of "The Canterbury Tales"; but, while his merits are being more and more acknowledged by foreign scholars, it may be questioned whether he has even yet attained a truly cosmopolitan fame.

Immediately below these very great writers comes a class which is plainly great, yet also plainly not supremely great, sometimes not great enough to be well known outside of their respective countries, but cherished by their countrymen as national glories. These are the authors one would never think of calling supreme, although one would as little think of calling them minor. We may call them, as is usual, simply "great writers"; for if we speak of them as constituting a "second class," as is sometimes done, we ignore the real distinction between them and the very great writers of whom mention has just been made. Of these really, but not supremely, or very great, authors every nation that has an important literature can point to several. No attempt at enumeration is here demanded, but we may be reasonably sure that both Catullus and Horace belong to the Roman list and Leopardi to the Italian. In English we have in this class such poets as Marlowe, Ben Jonson, Dryden, probably Pope and perhaps Gray, Burns, Coleridge, Keats, very probably Tennyson and Robert Browning, as well as Wordsworth, Byron, and Shelley, unless the partisans of the last group succeed in elevating one or more of them into the class of the very great poets. The reason one cannot speak more definitely is mainly to be found in the facts that not even yet have we settled the places of the eighteenth-century poets, and that the critics have too often spent their time in anathematizing one another instead of attending to their real business of attempting to reach such a consensus of opinion with regard to our classic authors as would correspond with, let us say, the consensus more or less obtaining in France. Still, scarcely any critic denies the existence of this class of great but not greatest writers, and the places of a majority of the names given are probably secure. This is enough for us, nor need we add the names of many corresponding masters of prose. Those of Charles Lamb and Hazlitt and Hawthorne will be sufficient.

As for the rest of the writers of a nation, for we have passed from the sphere of the cosmopolitan authors, critical usage is perplexingly various. Some critics have two or three classes, especially of poets, and speak of Dryden or Ben Jonson as the head of the second class. Some talk indefinitely of third and fourth classes. Some use the qualifying epithet "minor." In the midst of this confusion, which often puzzles students, and presumably general readers also, it may not be presumptuous to hazard the suggestion, — which harmonizes in part with a remark made by Sainte-Beuve to Matthew Arnold, — that it might be well to divide all worthy authors who fall below the class universally or usually called great into two classes as follows : —

First, important writers, — writers who have not power and range enough to be called great, although they often have a considerable range and have written some poetry, or a book or two, that may fairly be regarded as great ; — writers whom most of us will want to read in whole or in part because their genius, within well-defined limits, is genuine, and because they stand for something important in culture and in the history of literature and are also likely to interest in and for themselves. The poet William Collins will serve as an example. He did not write enough to be called great; his range of powers was not sufficiently wide; but he is regarded by those who know his work as a thoroughly genuine poet; he composed several poems like the "Ode to Evening" that are truly classic; and he is important because with Gray he helped to inaugurate the romantic movement among the eighteenth-century poets. To call Collins "minor" would be misleading, yet he is not great. He is, however, important, as is also, for example, in the realms of prose fiction, or at least of American fiction, our own first novelist, Charles Brockden Brown. To this class would probably belong those authors of large endeavor who with a little more genius or under more favorable circumstances, might have been indisputably great; such a man of letters, for example, as Robert Southey.

Secondly, the minor writers, — a class which should consist of writers of genuine quality, but of no conspicuous excellence, — poets, for instance, who are not mere versifiers, novelists who are not mere manufacturers of salable fiction, — authors in whose works any lover of books would be likely to find things well worth reading, but who might be neglected with no great loss. In other words, our class of minor writers should include those whom, without being impelled to blush at owning the fact, we might never find time to read, but who make a genuine appeal to many persons, and sometimes a strong appeal to a small class of readers. Such authors are very numerous and are sure to be increasingly numerous in the future, in view of the fact that so many men and women have become fairly equipped for the profession of letters. If concrete examples are needed, we may cite such a poet as the late Mr. Aubrey De Vere and such a novelist as Henry Kingsley. It should be remembered, however, that a minor or an occasional poet whose entire works we need not read, may write a poem we should all do well to read. Perhaps the name of the Rev. Charles Wolfe means nothing to most of us, but we do remember his

"Not a drum was heard, not a funeral note."

It is superfluous to add that below our minor writers fall the versifiers, the scribblers, the authors who won applause for a day, but were soon forgotten, and need not be revived. For these no classification is required here.

We do require, however, some practical tests to enable us to separate and place authors for our-

selves. I think that in the description or definition of what I proposed to call the important
and the minor writers, tests will be found for
determining who should belong to these classes;
but, after all, our main concern is with the
greatest and the great, and we can leave the
lesser authors to one side. Are there any tests
by which the greatest masters can be set apart;
that is, tests other than that of universal consent?
There seem to be.

If we examine the works of the supreme or
world-writers, we shall find that they have many
of their wonderful characteristics in common.

Their art, their technic is nearly always high
and uniform. We may open any page at ran-
dom and we shall discover some evidence —
whether a noble line — or a passage of supreme
metrical power and beauty — or marvellous turns
of expression or command of language — something that makes us exclaim, Here is a great
artist! In other words, the style of the world-
poet rarely flags. This is not true of most
of the merely great poets; it is not true, for
instance, of Wordsworth, or Byron, and, where
it is in the main true, as with Tennyson, there
is some unevenness of matter, some deficiency

of poetic energy, that counterbalances the per-
fection of style.

In the second place, the genius of none of
these supreme writers seems cramped; their
power is sovereign and sustained; their range
is either universal or very lofty. Homer, for
example, and Shakspere seem to set every
phase of life and character before us. They do
not really do this, but they seem to do it. Milton
and Dante, on the other hand, make up for their
lack of this universality by being able to rise to
sublime heights and to maintain their elevation.
They penetrate heaven itself. Goethe appears
to be universal in his knowledge of life and art,
and he succeeds in almost every form of literature. Balzac's acquaintance with human nature
seems portentously wide and deep. These things
are not true of the merely great authors. On
their own ground they may be great, nay, supreme; but off it their genius flags. Wordsworth, for instance, is almost unrivalled as a
nature and a reflective poet, but he had no dramatic genius, little humor, and slight sympathy
with many phases of life.

In the third place, each of these supreme
writers has achieved a long, sustained master-

piece, or a number of masterpieces.   The "Iliad,"
the "Odyssey," the "Œdipus Rex," the "Æneid,"
the "Divine Comedy," "Othello," "Hamlet," and
"Lear," "Paradise Lost," "Faust," — at once rise
before us.   The great writers, on the other hand,
when poets, rarely succeed when they attempt
long masterpieces, and, when novelists, rarely
give us a series of genuine masterpieces.   Wordsworth's "Excursion," Shelley's "Revolt of Islam"
and "Prometheus Unbound," Tennyson's "Idylls,"
Browning's "Ring and the Book," — are either
acknowledged failures as wholes or else have so
many critics and readers against them that the
question of their eminent greatness remains un-
decided.   But the world-writer has his practically
undisputed masterpiece, although he may have
much besides.   So, also, the very great writers
like Spenser have their undisputed masterpieces,
but these authors, as we have seen, lack some
of the characteristics of the world or supreme
writers.

In the fourth place, the world-writer, as his
name implies, has conquered the civilized world.
Whether he is read or not, his name is widely
known, and his place is yielded him ungrudgingly.
Milton is not very generally read, but his place is

secure, and if his name were mentioned to a cultivated Frenchman, the latter would know something about him. The Italians, on the other hand,
know very little about Wordsworth, while we do
know not a little about Dante. Most of us do
not know Leconte de Lisle, but the Frenchman,
while he does know Poe, retaliates by knowing
practically nothing about Bryant. As the world
is drawn closer together, this test of cosmopolitan
fame may cease to mean very much;[1] but at present
it is only supremely great authors, or exceptional
ones like Byron and Poe, who acquire really world-
wide fame, and the test is useful.

Our fifth and last test is one that applies also to
the other classes of writers, — the test of duration
of fame. But in the case of the genuine world-
writers a longer period of probation is normally
required. Victor Hugo, to use an example already
given, is probably a very great poet; but it will be
some years, perhaps some generations, before it
will be definitely known whether or not he has
risen to the dignity of being a world-poet.

[1] Note in this connection the increasing number of important
French studies of British and American writers. Two elaborate
volumes, one dealing with Poe and one with Hawthorne, have
appeared in the past few months.

There are obviously other tests that might be applied, but they are less concrete. World-writers are generally marked by supreme qualities in every respect, — supreme imagination, supreme range and copiousness of creative power, supreme command of language and rhythm, supreme seriousness and splendor of thought.

It would seem plain, in conclusion, that if we apply these tests, we ought to be able to tell quickly whether any given writer is worthy of the highest praise, and that we ought to make it almost a matter of duty not to indulge in hyperbolic laudation of any save the noblest authors.

A few words remain to be said about tests that may be applied to writers just below the highest rank, — to the writers I have proposed to denominate "very great." This, as we have seen, is a perplexing problem; but, if we will lay hold of the masterpiece test, it may help us. Any writer who has a long masterpiece or, in the case of prose, a series of books pronounced admirable by successive generations in his own country, and respected by competent critics abroad, seems entitled to rank among the very great writers, — the *dii minores* of literature. Thus, Spenser, Tasso,

Ariosto, and their peers belong to this class, and so, also, do novelists like Fielding. It is clear that none of these writers is characterized by universality of genius as Homer, Shakspere, Goethe are, nor by sublimity as Dante and Milton are; nor do any of them completely fulfil any of the other tests just given, although all do partially fulfil them. This class includes also, however, writers who have not a long masterpiece to their credit, but who can substitute for it a body of work of sufficient power, uniformity of merit, and important influence to be fairly equivalent to a masterpiece. The sonnets and canzoni of Petrarch, the lyrics of Heine, seem to entitle them to rank with or very near the writers of sustained and indubitable masterpieces. Thus we perceive that the fundamental test, both for the supreme writers and for the very great writers immediately below them, is excellence of sustained achievement.

Finally, as to the class of great writers, who are in the main of national importance only, we observe that they are separated from the classes above them by one fact, at least. They have no undisputed masterpiece, — indeed, they are generally marked by having an attempted masterpiece

which, on the whole, is a failure or only fairly
good, — nor have they a body of work of uniform and very high excellence. Wordsworth,
for instance, has his " Excursion " and " Prelude,"
when, if he is to rank with Spenser, he ought to
have something equivalent in both style and substance to the " Faerie Queene." He has in the
body of his poetry poems like " The Idiot Boy,"
and " Vaudracour and Julia," to offset the " Ode
to Duty " ; he has not left a body of poetry
marked by uniform excellence in its kind, such
as the sonnets of Petrarch. He has ups and
downs, and while his completely successful poems
and passages are probably better than anything
in Petrarch, his conspicuous failures more than
neutralize this advantage, and they have limited
his influence. But is not this another way of
saying that Wordsworth and writers of his class
often lack the power of self-criticism? They
leave us mixed work, because they cannot criticise themselves and cut out the poor work. This
seems to be a good test by which to separate these
poets from their superiors. A Spenser almost
invariably appears to have well in mind the essential principles and rules of his craft; a Wordsworth, a Browning, an Emerson, does not.

It is less easy to separate the great writers from those whom we may call merely important. The critics are at sea in the matter, but there are one or two tests that seem applicable. The great writer is supreme or nearly so on his own special ground, in his peculiar line — at least when he is at his best, and when his special line makes a genuine and wide appeal. Furthermore, in most cases, he has energy and versatility enough to try other lines of work, in some of which he achieves partial success. The merely important writer, on the other hand, is not supreme in any broad or really noteworthy sphere. Wordsworth is confessedly supreme as nature poet, but he also achieves success in reflective lyrics dealing with human life, and in classical themes. Byron is supreme as a poet of revolt, Browning as a courageous optimist, Keats as an apostle of pure beauty. But Collins and other important writers are either not supreme in anything, or else, as in the case of Thomas Campbell, are supreme only in a rather narrow class of compositions; in Campbell's case, in battle lyrics. Campbell's "Hohenlinden" and "Battle of the Baltic" are fine things; yet for two generations probably no one has thought that they may fairly

be set over against Wordsworth's supreme suc-
cesses as a nature poet.

But there is a limit to human endurance, and
a time or space limit ought to be set to all theo-
rizers. In view of these facts let me summarize
the points I have tried to make. I have tried
to show that it is proper to apply standards in
order to answer questions relating to approximately absolute and relative " greatness in literature," and that, whatever else " greatness in
literature " may mean, the truly great book or
writer must do something with us that is large,
important, influential, permanent, original, and
unique, and must do it either in the sphere of
our emotions or in that of our intelligence, or
in both. I have tried to show also that the
universal tendency to rank writers and the forms
of literature is founded on a law of our nature,
and that the application of collective standards
of judgment will enable us to classify authors
in a useful and not too arbitrary way. I have
tried to show that writers worthy of attention
may be conveniently divided according as they
are supreme, very great, great, important, and
minor. I have distinguished these classes from
one another, and have endeavored to give prac-

tical tests by which any reader may at least begin to discriminate in his reading.

It is scarcely necessary to insist that all that has been said is intended to be suggestive merely. Even if the classification attempted has been made on correct lines, it needs filling out and requires many qualifications. There are writers who can only with difficulty be classified under this or any other scheme. Is Herrick, for instance, a great or only an important poet? Then, again, by the classification here suggested, a writer might be put in a rather high class, yet certain obvious defects might make it very questionable whether his rank ought not to be reduced. And we must always remember that any scheme of classification is bad if it tends to make our judgments hard and fast, if it induces us to think that we can stick a pin through a writer and ticket him as an entomologist does an insect.[1] But if we use such a

[1] See in this connection the curious essay on "The Balance of the Poets" by Mark Akenside, based on a French attempt to "balance" the painters. On a scale of twenty he marked Ariosto, Dante, Horace, Pindar, Pope, Racine, and Sophocles thirteen; that is, five below the marks assigned to Homer and Shakspere. This particular exercise of the "Pleasures of the Imagination" may be found in the New Brunswick (New Jersey) edition of Akenside, 1808.

scheme intelligently, it may prove useful, if only by stimulating us to candid objections, for candid objections imply honest thought, and honest thought on such a noble subject as literature cannot but be beneficial. On the other hand, if any one finds that ranking and weighing authors and books tends to diminish his enjoyment of them, he may safely relegate discussions like the present to any sort of limbo he pleases, provided he does not intolerantly insist, as some good people are too likely to do, that his way of approaching literature is the only one permitted to rational mortals.

II

A WORD FOR THE SMALLER AUTHORS AND FOR POPULAR JUDGMENT

[The substance of two short papers contributed to *The Churchman* for December 4 and 18, 1897.]

II

A WORD FOR THE SMALLER AUTHORS AND FOR POPULAR JUDGMENT

I TRUST that in the preceding paper I have sufficiently guarded myself against any imputation that I consider literature as something that can be accurately measured by hard and fast rules. I really do not think that there is any instrument by which one can tell the amount of greatness in a particular book with the ease and certainty with which one can tell the number of degrees to which steam has heated our deadly offices and apartments. Nor do I actually range authors on my shelves according to their size as though they were bushel, peck, quart, and pint measures. But, although I may not have left any such impression, I may very possibly have failed to say enough on two points closely related to the discussion just ended — if, indeed, any such discussion ever is ended. I have not dwelt sufficiently on the uses of the "smaller" authors, whether, adopting the classification I have suggested, we call them "important" or "minor"; and I have not said enough in regard to the adequacy, within certain limits, of popular judgment in matters literary and artistic. On these two points I should like to dwell for a moment.

I. SMALLER AUTHORS AND THEIR USES

It is surely good advice that our great critics bestow, when they tell us, as they all do, that we should live with the classics. That is, of course, what we mean to do, but it is emphatically what the majority of us fail to do for the whole or the greater portion of our lives. Some of us, although we may legitimately call ourselves readers, do not pretend to do more than glance through a few standard authors and read a few essays or books about them. Others of us are glad if we can say that we have read through once the chief poets and some of the great prose writers of the literatures to which we have access. A few of us endeavor to keep up fairly well with contemporary books and writers and at the same time to reread now and then a standard author. An almost infinitesimal fraction of us obeys the critical mandate, and lives, even in part, with the classics.

This is not to be wondered at so much as it is
to be deplored. Contemporary literature has the
potent voice of fashion on its side. It has, too,
the siren voice of discovery, of appropriation.
The classics belong to every one ; few or no standard authors can be appropriated except after years
of patient labor. A contemporary writer is always
more or less in need of a prophet, a herald, an
interpreter. Then, again, although the true classics
exist for all men and all times, it is hard to persuade ourselves that they are as modern, as " up-to-
date " as Mr. Hardy's last novel[1] or Mr. Kipling's
last volume of poems. Whether it be true or not,
we at least imagine that the classics require more
intellectual effort on our part for their proper
understanding and appreciation than is necessary
in the case of the latest novel or biography of
which we have read a review. In fine, the recent
novel comes to us ; we have to go to the classics.
Hence it is that we cut new pages instead of add-
ing thumb-marks to old ones ; and hence it is that
some of us are even heterodox enough to smile
when critics preach the classics to us. Fortunately,

[1] When these words were written, it was still possible to speak of
Mr. Hardy's last novel as one that would soon be his next to the
last.

or unfortunately, not many of us are yet sufficiently bold to enter with Mr. Howells and Mr. Garland upon a veritable "battle of the books" and to bear a lance against the redoubtable champions of the looming past.[1]

If all this be true, it would seem that it is a work of supererogation to plead the cause of the writers whom we designate as "smaller." If the classics fail to receive proper recognition, of what avail will it be to call attention to the subtle beauties of any minor poet that sleeps in the dust of a graveyard or a library? If contemporary literature already has the upper hand, is not the minor poet of the "living present" thoroughly able to take care of himself? In view of this dilemma, it would seem that no one could seriously undertake to discuss minor poets, taken either separately or collectively, unless he were one of those specialists so common now whose main excuse for writing is, not that their subject is worth knowing, but that it is so little known.

Dilemmas, however, are not always such dangerous forks to the writer who loves his theme as

---

[1] I had in mind "Criticism and Fiction" and "Crumbling Idols." Romance still clings to the idols, which still stand firmly on their pedestals.

those of Caudium were to the Roman legionaries. Logic has been known to go down before volubility, and it is always possible to restate propositions in such a way as to lead imperceptibly to conclusions quite different from those formerly reached. Perhaps, after all, when the great critics tell us we must live with the classics, their injunction is not to be taken as a universal imperative. Granted that we had the time and the inclination, would it be possible for us to live always with the classics without experiencing some of the effects of *ennui*, not to say repulsion? With the exception of the two universal poets, Shakspere and Homer, if even they are to be excepted, could we find in the classics an answer to our every mood? Hardly, if we mean by the classics the more important, the larger writers of the past. There is, of course, a sense in which Matthew Prior is a classic. He is, in the judgment of some of us, the greatest English writer of *vers de société*. His position in our literature is well defined and secure. But, in another sense of the word, Prior can scarcely be termed a classic, because his work does not reach a sufficiently high level of moral and intellectual greatness. He is plainly a "smaller" poet, but just as plainly one that has his uses.   However much we ought to study and love Shakspere, there are surely times when we can well afford to read Prior, and it is a pleasure to love him always.

If this be true of Prior and of other poets of the same category, it is clear that we need fear the horns of no dilemma.   We may cheerfully grant that we ought to live with the classics far more than we do, and that the critics are right in devoting most of their time and talents to praising and elucidating the larger and more splendid writers of the past.   But we may hold at the same time that there are authors of less worth who should be sojourned with for a season by all persons fond of good literature, and that the hospitable virtues of these writers should be praised and set forth by grateful critics.   Because, as in the case of the classics, few contemporary readers will be affected by this praise is no reason why it should not be given often and ungrudgingly.   It is even possible that through this praise of authors, especially of minor poets, who answer to particular moods and desires, some of us may be led to a study and appreciation of the genuine classics.   Not infrequently general consensus of praise alienates those whom it was intended to attract.   Like erring Guineveres with perfect Arthurs, we find too late that we have rebelled against what has been universally extolled, although it has been all along what our higher nature craved. If, however, we become attracted to what is really good, though not the highest, we may pass on by slow steps to an appreciation of the greatest and best; not by quick revulsion, as was the case with the guilty queen who tampered with crime. If, with a taste for good literature implicit in us, we yet consent to defile or enervate our minds with what is foul or frivolous, we shall probably some day revolt from our mental slavery when it is too late. Let us, then, cherish the "smaller" writers who appeal to special tastes and aptitudes of a wholesome sort, and we may be sure that in a majority of cases we shall be sooner or later drawn into the company of those who love the classics. For it is with literature as it is with religion and morals. One of the most effective ways to render a man fit and likely to practise the heroic virtues is to inure him in the practice of the homely virtues. All sermons cannot deal with patriotism, and self-abnegation of the Sidneyan type, and the like exalted themes; some sermons must deal with filial obedience, neighborly charity, and kindred homely virtues. Just so it is well for critics occasionally to cease preaching the classics and to invite us to learn to love the lesser writers.

II. POPULAR JUDGMENT AND EXPERT OPINION

Turning now to the second of the topics named above, we are at once brought face to face with the fact that there has long existed with a certain class of critics a profound distrust of popular judgment in matters of literature and art. "The people at large," say these literary and artistic mandarins in effect, "has only coarse and rudimentary tastes and is continually bestowing its affection upon unworthy objects. It prefers the late General Lew Wallace to Mr. George Meredith, and not at all on patriotic considerations. It cannot appreciate Wagner, and has never really given its suffrage to Browning. We will therefore ignore the likes and dislikes of the people, will form ourselves into a coterie, and will write criticism for the benefit of one another — that is to say, of the elect."

Unfortunately, there is a large element of truth in the reasons given consciously or held unconsciously by the mandarins for the exclusive attitude they assume. The popular taste is often extremely crude, and public favorites are often distinctly unworthy of praise. Two facts, however, should be remembered by the fastidious critics who seek to shun the *ignotum vulgus*. The first is that, if reasoned with patiently, the public is almost sure to come around in the end to right ways of thinking. The second is that some of the greatest writers and artists have long since become genuinely popular, which could not have happened if the public were totally devoid of taste. Italians of all degrees of cultivation are said to read and love Dante, and the same thing is approximately true of Englishmen with regard to Shakspere. Mere lip-service to great poets and artists counts, indeed, for nothing, since your public is generally willing to acknowledge that a man must be great if it hears his name often enough; but genuine fondness for a great author does count for much in any proper estimate of the æsthetic capacity of the masses.

Critics have, to be sure, frequently recognized the fact that certain great writers make a universal appeal; but they nearly always draw from it conclusions relative rather to the power of the writer than to the inherent capacity of the public to appreciate what is largely noble and true. Yet that the public is normally capable of this sort

of appreciation seems to be proved by political
no less than by literary history. The American
people as a whole recognized the large nobleness
and sincerity of Washington's character even during his lifetime — recognized it in much the same
way as the Italian peasant recognizes the large
nobleness and sincerity of his national poet. Just
so in spiritual matters the large nobleness and
truth of the great historic religions are recognized
by the lowly as well as by those in high places
whose advantages have naturally given them a
wider culture.   It was for this reason that in
Christian England Bunyan's " Pilgrim's Progress "
became almost immediately a favorite book among
the poor, and was enabled, after Cowper's day, to
live down the neglect and contempt of the educated
classes.

As I have said, the mandarins are not ignorant
of the facts just cited, but it would certainly look
as if they failed to draw one salutary lesson from
them.   This lesson, if I am not mistaken, may
be condensed as follows : If a writer or artist has
been before the public for a period sufficiently
long to allow all mere temporary aberrations of
judgment to be eliminated, and still fails of genuine popularity, then the inference ought to be

that, unless some definite reason not properly chargeable to the man or his work can be assigned for the continued lack of popularity, the writer or artist in question — Landor, for example — ought not to be regarded as possessing sufficient nobleness and sincerity of character, as expressed in his work, to be worthy of a place among the greatest masters.

The position here taken may become plainer if it is couched in other words. Are we not bound by the teaching of history and experience to presume that in the long run the judgment of the public with regard to the greatness of the men of a very high order of endowments, not adequately recognized by contemporaries, will coincide with that of the few far-sighted critics who proclaimed their glory before it was generally acknowledged ? If such a presumption is fair, it follows that if the public continues obdurate to the claims made by critics for certain writers, the critics are mistaken, at least in part. This is certainly the stand an optimist ought to take; for if large nobleness and truth fail in the end, except under very special circumstances, to win the admiration and recognition of the masses of men, the future of the race is dark indeed.

I believe that the critics will have to accept this conclusion at some not distant day. It will simply mean that a few special favorites of the mandarins will have to be set in a lower niche in the Temple of Fame; for the supreme and the very great and even the great writers, as a rule, appeal to the people as well as to the critics. No thoughtful man will deny the value of expert opinion, and it is plainly expert opinion which does most to place the secondary men of genius where they belong. When large nobleness and truth are absent, the verdict of the public is of no great moment, and the more minute study of the expert tells with full force.   Botticelli, therefore, if I may be allowed to draw my examples from an art in which I am certainly anything but expert, may take a secondary place undisputed if the experts decide that he is entitled to it; but it would seem that the critics of art may as well give up trying to place him alongside of or above Titian and Raphael. Apparently he has not the large and permanent qualities that win the suffrage of the public; hence he does not belong of right to the very highest rank of painters.

There is, however, one point that needs to be noticed in this connection. It happens sometimes, though rarely, that the form of expression chosen by a master of the highest rank becomes, for reasons over which he has no control, somewhat repellent to the masses in later generations. When this is the case, as it partly is, for example, with Milton, the consensus of the best current critical opinion with that of past critical and popular opinion is practically sufficient to establish the rank of the writer or artist in question. In this case it will be observed that the large nobility and sincerity which have been posited are not as a rule denied; they are merely obscured by the form of expression which has become obsolete. In the case of the famous painter just used as an example, the large nobility and sincerity required do not seem to be present in sufficient quantity to impress the public as they do in the cases of Titian and Raphael. Something may, however, be said with regard to the popular inability to appreciate such an artist on account of certain impediments to a full understanding of his form of expression; and if this be true, it is possible that what has just been said with regard to Milton, holds good also of him. But certainly the sneers and the pharisaical bearing of the mandarins toward the public cannot be justified on any grounds.

III

THE AIMS AND METHODS OF LITERARY STUDY

[Read before a few students of English at Princeton University, November, 1901.   Delivered before the Missouri Teachers' Association at Kansas City, December, 1901.   Published in *The Sewanee Review*, January, 1904.]

III

THE AIMS AND METHODS OF
LITERARY STUDY

THAT within the past ten years there has been in this country a marked increase of interest in literature and literary studies is a statement which will scarcely be disputed by any person occupied with such matters. The growth of literary clubs, especially among women, .the emphasis laid upon English literature in primary and secondary schools, the work done by university extension lecturers, and, particularly, the trend in our colleges and universities from purely philological to literary courses may be cited as evidences that the phenomenon exists. If these evidences are not sufficient, we may add to them the development of libraries, of the publishing business, and of literary departments in the daily newspapers. That this interest is more intense or more deep-seated than was the similar interest manifested in New England during the days of the Transcendental Movement need be neither affirmed nor denied; but it is naturally far more widespread, and it is certainly an advance upon whatever popular interest in literature was displayed during the two decades that followed the civil war.

The causes of the phenomenon need not be investigated too curiously. Throughout the world our generation has been critical rather than creative, and a critical age is in the main only another name for an epoch of literary studies. Then, to go somewhat deeper, great accumulation of wealth and great accompanying desire for luxury and for culture, as a fit adjunct of luxury, coinciding with an era of self-consciousness and of democratic development, must make for an increase in studies which themselves make for refinement, for personal distinction, and for relief from ennui. The very confusion of our age, which has probably affected its creative work disastrously, has driven many men and women to pursuits of a literary nature as to a kind of haven, even if this same confusion has often rendered their studies mainly nugatory, except as a moral sedative.

But while this increase of popular interest in literature and in literary studies may be taken for

granted and while its causes may remain uninvestigated, it hardly seems wise not to consider somewhat carefully the aims and methods of the eager
students of literature we see on all sides, and to
compare their ends and means with those ideal
ends and means which, after a due survey of
the field, we may set up for ourselves and for
them. Such a setting up of ideals for other
people is always hazardous; but if our methods
of reasoning are both inductive and deductive, if
we rely upon observation as much as upon theory,
and upon common sense as much as upon either,
we shall be able, perhaps, to reach some useful results. What, then, seem to be the aims of
students of literature, as to-day we see them in
this country applying themselves to their chosen
and delightful work? In answering this question
a rough classification of such students will be
serviceable.

The most obvious division is into professional
students and amateurs or dilettantes, but it is easy
and necessary to divide further. Professional
students of literature fall, I think, into much the
same classes as other professional men. There
are those who are born with an aptitude for letters, who become successful critics, noted teachers

of literature, or men of letters devoting a portion of their creative energy to criticism, such as
Mr. Howells and Mr. Henry James for our own
epoch, or as Ben Jonson and John Dryden among
the elder writers. These are the leaders occupy-
ing, except when they are great geniuses, much
the same position as the more eminent clergymen,
lawyers, and physicians do. In the rank and file
are found the minor critics, a majority of the
teachers of literature, most of the itinerant lecturers on literary subjects, and the book reviewers.
These correspond with the safe, respectable prac-
titioners whom most of us are glad to employ when
we are ill. Below these, as in every other profession, come the utter mediocrities, the failures and
the quacks, about whom we need say nothing.

The amateurs are harder to classify. At their
head, however, plainly stands the literary virtuoso,
the man of refined taste who lives in an atmos-
phere of culture, and who, if he writes, is almost
sure to illuminate whatever subject he touches.
He frequently has other than literary interests,
and he never has hard and fast obligations to
publishers, readers, or students. A good type of
such a virtuoso is Horace Walpole ; another and
very different type is Edward FitzGerald, the

translator of Omar Khayyám, who, if he had been less of a recluse, would now probably be ranked among the greater English critics. Below the virtuoso comes what we may call loosely the cultivated man or woman who has acquired through natural instinct and training a love of books and a fairly wide knowledge of them, often considerable in one or more departments. We all know many such persons, although in busy America they are doubtless proportionally fewer in number than in England or in France. Below these come the serious and honorable aspirants for culture, the men and women who, in spite of meagre educational opportunities and of lives full of other and more pressing cares and duties, seize every chance and means of cultivating themselves. University, college, and high school students, who may, in a short time, belong to one of the other groups already mentioned, must, at some period in their career, be numbered with these aspirants for culture. Finally, in the lowest class, fall the men and women who are entitled only to the unpleasant designation of smatterers, of whom, as of the quacks, we need take no further notice.

With regard, now, to the aims of all lovers of literature who are worthy of being in any sense classed as students, it is obvious that from many points of view the most inspiring are those cherished by the great critics and men of letters to whom literature, in some blended words of Keats, is a thing of beauty, and therefore a thing of truth and a joy forever. But because these men are as much born to literary studies as Plato, about whose young lips the bees clustered, was born to golden eloquence, their aims and methods, while serviceable as ideal standards, must always be unattainable by the large majority; and this is true also of the aims and methods of the virtuoso, although these, while honorable, are not fully inspiring because they are less purely philanthropic in character, less founded on the noble idea of service to fellow-men. It follows that it is with the aims of the majority of literary students, whether professional or amateur, that we are most concerned; and in pursuing this subject let us ask and try to answer a fundamental question : Why do or why should men study literature ?

If one is born with a bent to such study, it is a sufficient answer to our question to assert the existence of the bent; for we may assume that literature is a worthy object of knowledge, and that all worthy objects of knowledge deserve to be studied by chosen spirits. But there are few chosen spirits, and students of literature are very numerous. Is not this because there is implanted in all persons endowed with spiritual aspirations a desire, not merely of self-distinction (smatterers and mediocrities have this), but of drawing nearer to ideal beauty, truth, and goodness, preferably in some form of combination? And because in genuine literature ideal beauty, truth, and goodness are found in combination, expressed through the medium of language, with which, when it is our own, we are more familiar than we are with the mediums of expression employed by the sculptor, the painter, and the musician, do not more men and women seek the ideal through literature than through any other means save religion? Students of literature are numerous, then, and increasingly numerous, because they find through literature their easiest access to the ideal.

But if a more or less conscious aspiration for the most accessible ideal be the basic reason for the popular interest in literary studies, which we have posited, it would seem to follow that the aims and methods of the teacher and the student of literature ought to make for the attainment of ideal truth, beauty, and goodness in the fullest

possible measure. The introduction of any antagonistic aim or method must necessarily militate
against the attainment of the central purpose for
which, according to our reasoning, literary studies
are begun.   An important consequence ensues.
We do not draw nearer to ideal beauty, truth, and
goodness in combination if we give the acquisition
of mere knowledge a disproportionate place in our
aims and methods.   Knowledge helps us to attain
truth, but it does not prompt to, although it does
direct, the realization of goodness in conduct and
the appreciation of beauty.   We do not truly
study literature unless through our studies we gain
wisdom in contradistinction to mere knowledge,
and unless we also develop our æsthetic faculties
and, what is far more to the purpose, become
better men and women.   Hence knowledge in
relation to literature should always occupy an
ancillary position — it should be the handmaiden
charged with ushering us into the presence of the
ideal.   But what have our teachers and professors
of literature, our editors of school and college
texts, our writers of learned monographs and
manuals, and finally our promoters of literary clubs
and lecture courses to say about themselves in these
premises?   Do they not too frequently make mere

knowledge the be-all and the end-all of their work? It is so easy for teacher and pupil to add fact to fact and call it studying literature — whereas in its best estate such attainment of knowledge about literature is only a means to culture, not culture itself; while in its worst estate it is a positive bar to culture and its pleasures.

Just here we may note a distinct advance that has been made in the past ten years. Most of the literary work that was done in our colleges and universities fell under the department of English and, in consequence, under the direction of men who, in general, were trained philologists. What attention they gave to the literature produced by Englishmen and Americans after the year 1600 was in the main perfunctory; and although there was no lack of great authors and books prior to that year, these were seldom treated save as storehouses of linguistic facts.

Now philology [1] is far from being an uninteresting study, and it is, of course, most important, whether considered in itself or in its relations with history and literature and other subjects of human inquiry. But unless admirably handled by the

[1] It is almost needless to say that the word is used here in its narrower, not in its larger sense.

teacher, philology, like any other science, however valuable it may be in other respects, is less available than literature as a means to culture. It tends to aid us but slightly in our approach to the ideal, whereas literature should aid us greatly. Fortunately during the past ten years this fact has been more and more recognized in American colleges and universities, until, in some institutions indeed, the balance has been tipped almost unfairly against philology. In England this does not seem to be the case; yet there a great amount of literary training has always been obtainable through the best of mediums, the Greek and Latin classics.

But while all our institutions of learning, schools and libraries, as well as colleges and universities, afford better facilities for the study of literature than they did a decade ago, the improvement is not great enough to warrant a large amount of self-approbation. Philology no longer stalks about in borrowed plumes; but the history of literature, which is a branch of culture-history, is frequently studied to the exclusion of literature itself; and when great poetry and great prose are put before the student, this is often done so mechanically and with such a lack of proportion in the treatment that the cause of culture is not greatly subserved. For example, deadly methods of analysis, supplemented by a terrifying apparatus of largely irrelevant questions, are daily applied in our schoolrooms to poems which were written to stir the emotions, not perplex the minds of unoffending children. In other words, the letter of literature is diligently conned, but the delicate spirit of literature — I was going to say — escapes both the teacher and the pupil — but it really does not escape at all. It remains, as it were, an Ariel imprisoned in the tree of knowledge, waiting for a Prospero to give it freedom. Again, through over-emphasis and under-emphasis in their treatment of writers, our teachers and professors and lecturers and critics are giving the world of students and readers very narrow and distorted views as to the scope of that literature which is one of the main glories of the Anglo-Saxon race. I have often found that the names of important seventeenth and eighteenth century writers meant absolutely nothing, not to a schoolboy or an undergraduate, but to a graduate student who intended to make the teaching of literature his life-work.

Perhaps just here, even at the risk of somewhat attenuating the strength of whatever arguments this discussion may involve, it will not be amiss for me to dwell for a moment upon what seem to be faults of our professional teaching and studying of literature that demand correction.

One, as hinted above, is the preponderating part in literary teaching and criticism played by analysis. It is the fashion with many critics to dwell upon the internal rather than upon the external features of a piece of literature, to dilate upon its qualities rather than upon what it is as a whole, to treat it as something to be dissected rather than to discuss its general effects upon readers at large and its position in the body of national or world literature. To put it otherwise, their criticism tends to be analytic and subjective rather than synthetic and objective. There is much room, indeed, for such criticism, since it obviously serves to bring out beauties that would otherwise lie hidden, and to intensify our interest in the writer and his work. Yet it is very questionable whether such analytic criticism should occupy so prominent a part or come so early in our literary training. After all, it seems mainly to ask and answer the question, Why does this author appeal to us in such and such a way? But this is a question more important to a writer than to a reader. If we are undertaking to write poetry, by all means let us analyze great poetry and try to seize the secret of its power. If we are readers, however, it is perhaps better to try first to answer the questions, How has this writer affected others — that is, What ought we to expect to find in him? and, How does this writer compare with others in his class — that is, Should we devote ourselves to him as much as to some other and greater man?

It is at once plain that we have here in somewhat disguised forms the two well-defined methods of criticism for which those distinguished Frenchmen, M. Lemaître and M. Brunetière, and other critics ranged behind each of them, have long been doing battle — methods of criticism which, in fact, have been in the world for ages and to which we give the names Impressionist and Academic. It is plain also that my complaint is that of late, and especially in our teaching of literature, we have not been giving academic criticism — the criticism of judgment — due consideration; that we have been overpartial to the criticism of interpretation, which tends more or less to be impressionist in character. I am constantly reading and hearing criticisms of books that make me wonder whether the analyzer has ever put together the qualities he discovers, whether he has ever grasped as a whole the piece of literature with which he is dealing. He talks of sublimity, charm, love of nature, *et cetera*, until I wonder whether he is not in the position of the proverbial person who cannot see the wood for the trees. It seems to me that it would be much more logical and profitable for our critics and teachers to begin with the criticism of judgment — for example, to judge a poem as a whole; to get its position, as near as one can in the poet's own works, in the class of poems to which it belongs, in the literature of the nation, and finally, if it be worth the pains, in the literature of the world. Then it would be logical and proper to pass to the more intensive method of analysis and interpretation, which would increase both our knowledge and our enjoyment. It is true that no one can entirely separate these two methods of criticising. We analyze somewhat when we are trying to determine what a poem or book stands for as a whole. But I am quite sure that in our school and college classes we give too much place to the analytic or interpretive method, with the result that, when we ought to be getting wide views of literature and life, we learn to know a few works of a few writers only, trusting to time to introduce us to the rest. Time, however, is more like a slave driver than a master of ceremonies, and thus nine out of ten of us are confined throughout our lives to a mere hearsay acquaintance even with great authors, much more with minor ones.

From what I have just said, the reader will not be surprised to learn that I am somewhat sceptical as to the good results of much of the teaching of literature based on the so-called series of English classics, though I have contributed to such series myself;[1] that I am not altogether convinced that the excessive attention paid to Shakspere in schools and colleges is wise; that I doubt very much whether it is profitable to spend a term or a year on any one writer or small group of writers, unless it can be done in connection with courses that give a wide survey of the form of literature that is being studied; that I am inclined to think that

[1] See the sixth paper for a fuller discussion of this matter.

all so-called "laboratory courses" in literature should be accompanied, as they are in the case of the natural sciences, by lectures that serve not merely to present the subject as a whole but also to set it in its historical and philosophical relations with other subjects of human inquiry and with life itself. I know that it is much easier to teach and learn a minute division of a subject, and that for purposes of imparting methods of study — that is, for graduate instruction — such division is often absolutely necessary. But I cannot perceive that our specialistic training is giving us the grasp upon literature that many of our untrained fathers and mothers had, and I think it is time for us to ask ourselves where we are and whither we are tending.

Nor should our queries be confined to the whereabouts and the whitherwards of the teachers of literature. The literary specialists who furnish us with admirably detailed studies and monographs often lead us astray by the importance they give to very minor writers or to small literary movements, and cause us to blunder by applying to literature that historic or, perhaps better, that pedantic estimate against which Matthew Arnold warned us. Yet the monographs and dissertations continue to come out, and we may easily swamp ourselves in the minutiæ of scholarship, while philosophic criticism goes begging for adherents, and comparative literature attracts too few students. As a result, even the nomenclature of the art of criticism is at sixes and sevens. Think, for example, of how little definiteness attaches to the term " lyric." So also the application of the theory of evolution to the study of literature is yet in its infancy. Where, for instance, will one find a consistent and full account of the evolution of that highest form of lyric, the ode? No wonder that the students of the sciences look severely askance at us when we pose as anything but amateurs. No wonder that the late Mr. Freeman, the historian, spoke scornfully of us as chatterers about poor Harriet Shelley, or that Mark Twain, after reading Professor Dowden's treatment of the relations between Shelley and his unfortunate first wife, was constrained like a knight-errant to enter the lists against the biographer. In nine cases out of ten, when we have not chattered, we have been grubbing ; yet we are neither sparrows nor worms.

Still, even if all that I have just said by way of adverse criticism be well founded, it is undeniable that a great advance has been made in the study of literature viewed as a constituent element in the academic curriculum; it is equally undeniable that in this country in matters of culture we can never afford to confine our attention to the academic class. As we have seen, there is an immense and increasing amount of self-cultivation in literature being attempted by American men and women of all classes. What are the aims and methods of these people?

I am not sure that their aims are not often higher, I will not say than those of teachers generally, — for I believe that the aims of our teachers are very high, — but higher than those of the apparently more fortunate college student or professor, or of the minor critical writers and lecturers. These very frequently appear to me to be turning to the study of literature as a means for obtaining a livelihood or as a peculiarly pleasant and easy method of exploiting a popular taste. We may posit, to be sure, in most cases, a bent for literary studies; but very frequently a fair salary, a good social position, and a long vacation are more in evidence as motives to the assumption of a literary calling as college teacher than any *œstrus* sent by the gods to goad the aspiring spirit up the steep and arduous heights of culture. And as for the popular lecturer, it would at least appear easy for a soulful young man to persuade himself that it is his life-work to lecture on Dante to a group of adoring women at so many dollars per head.

On the other hand, if we eliminate the dabbling in literature done by men and women who think that a certain show of culture is desirable, it seems to me that the aims of a considerable portion of the amateur students of literature in America are distinctly high, at least from a moral point of view. They are trying to elevate themselves by contact with the ideal, and there can be no higher individual aim. There is a tremendously impressive earnestness to be observed among such literary workers in every section of the country. And where this strenuousness is not visible, there is often a quiet, dignified pursuit of culture, though perhaps along narrow lines, to be found among persons whose vocations hardly suggest literary or artistic proclivities. It is plain, however, that all aspiration for self-culture is more or less lacking in that altruism which is to be seen, in some measure at least, in the aims of teachers and of other professional students, and that, as a rule, the methods of the amateur are less well-grounded and comprehensive than those of his fellow-worker.

It is desirable in this connection to comment briefly upon the increasing number of "collectors" to be found in America. The treasures in the shape of rare manuscripts and books contained in the libraries of some of our rich men, and in many cases made accessible to the student with unparalleled generosity, are startling to the uninitiated in these matters. That such collectors, especially those who delight in rich bindings and extra illustrations, are always men of true culture, it would be hazardous to assert; but many of them are, and any manifestation of a love of the beautiful or even of respect for the instrumentalities of culture is of great importance in educating the taste of the public. But we must not rest satisfied with witnessing the raids made by our millionaires upon the collections of Europe or with chronicling the growth of bibliophile societies, excellent work though these are doing. We must be insistent in our demands that our great cities one and all range themselves with Boston in the zealous formation of libraries in which the student can find practically all the originals and facsimiles he needs for the most minute investigation.[1]

From what has been said it would seem to follow that the aims of the professional student of literature need to be made more ideal and less practical, his methods more flexible and less mechanical, while the aims of the amateur should be made more altruistic and his methods less nebulous. How are these ends best to be attained ?

I know of no better way than for the one class of literary students to keep constantly in mind the aims of the other class, and to consider carefully and partly adopt its methods of study. This is precisely what they are not doing at present. The critic is much too likely to smile with condescension at literary opinions advanced by people who have not read so many hundreds of books as he has. On the other hand, the literary amateur or the cultivated reader is much too likely to think that the critic is the slave of his own rules or a mere dry-as-dust whose opinion is pedantic and

---

[1] With regard to the acquisition of facsimiles upon a large scale, see the letters by Professor Charles M. Gayley and others which *The Evening Post* has recently been publishing.

absurd. This is especially the case among Anglo-
Saxons, who as a race have cherished a distrust of
criticism, apparently on the principle that, as an
Englishman's house is his castle, so his opinions
ought to be surrounded by a moat of ignorance
and prejudice. In other words, our two classes
of literary workers are in many respects sundered;
whereas it appears, as I have just said, that each
class should consider carefully and partly adopt
the aims and methods of the other.

The professional student is constantly in danger
of forgetting that the spirit of literature, not its
mere external form or garb, should be the true
object of his study. He forgets that study means
zeal for, as well as application to, an object, and
he is too seldom zealous for that ideal of truth,
beauty, and goodness in combination which genuine literature embodies. The better class of
amateurs, however, the men and women of
acquired or accumulating culture, are nearly
always more or less alive to the value of literature
as a means to lift themselves from the plane of
the real to that of the ideal. They are less likely
than the professional student to use literary studies
either as a practical means of livelihood or as an
exercise of their purely intellectual faculties. On

the other hand, the amateur, to whom literature is generally a "side issue," a matter apart, is likely to make it a matter of merely personal gratification. He seldom has to consider the interests of others, whether as an expounder or a popularizer or what we may call a literary missionary. He can hold his own opinions regardless of what others think, can be as erratic as he pleases, can be selfish, and all the while can fall back upon the favorite maxim of the Englishman, which is often expressed in Latin, "*De gustibus non est disputandum*," there is no disputing about tastes. This selfish, nonaltruistic attitude toward something that is essentially noble and ideal cannot be good for any one. Perhaps there ought to be no disputing about tastes, but there ought to be calm discussion of them, and we should endeavor to make our own taste and that of our neighbor relish the highest possible forms of literature and art. Hence it is well for the amateur to do what the professional student must always do, — consider the tastes of others, determine what has been the verdict of cultivated readers in the past with regard to the relative ranking of the various forms of literature and other cognate matters ; in short, equip himself to pursue his favorite subject in a critical and not in a purely desultory and inconsequential manner.

But we have passed, almost without knowing it, from a discussion of aims to a discussion of methods. The methods of the professional student are naturally such as we loosely denominate critical, whether or not his bias be toward history or linguistics or æsthetics, or his allegiance be given to the academic or the impressionist school. There is no time to discuss the best methods by which the critic or judge appraises the value of a work of literary art; what mainly concerns us is the fact that the chief danger which confronts the critic or the teacher is that his methods may easily become mechanical. Against this danger his best safeguard will be found, I believe, in an application of the less hard-and-fast methods of study pursued by the amateur. The professional student should relax his mind by a limited following of his own bent in reading, by an indulgence at times in uncritical enthusiasm, by a frequent surrender of his spirit to the appeals of the ideal. He should remember the adage about the ever-stretched bow, and not forget that he has a soul as well as an intellect. On the contrary, the amateur has much to gain by endeavor-

ing to catch something of that balanced judgment,
that free play of mind which will always be found to
characterize the true critic. He should not weight
himself down with learning or cease to enjoy what
he is laboring to apprehend; but he should endeavor to impart some system to his reading, and
he should avoid nebulosity and inconsistency in
the judgments he forms upon literary topics. For
example, he should not without a murmur wade
through the theology with which Dante overloads
"The Divine Comedy," and inveigh against that
with which Milton overloads "Paradise Lost."
Above all, he should avoid the prevailing lack of
critical catholicity. He should strive, for instance,
to appreciate both Byron and Shelley, and not
decry the one in order to laud the other.

The mention of Byron leads naturally to a consideration of the only other point I wish to make in
this paper. It is Byron, of all modern English poets
— indeed, of all modern Englishmen save Scott —
who has had most influence upon the Continental
public; it is Byron of all modern English poets of
eminence, toward whom most opposition, not to
say rancor, has been displayed by native critics.
Of late it has been growing more and more plain,
I think, that British and American depreciation of

Byron has ridiculously overshot the mark; that while certain technical defects, not obvious to foreigners, must be emphasized by Anglo-Saxon critics, — not for the purpose of running down Byron, but for the sake of warning present and future poets against his mistakes, — the point of view of the foreign critics is far more sound than that of almost any critic writing in English save Matthew Arnold. Whether this be true or not, it is abundantly clear that no student of literature, whether professional or amateur, can afford either to ignore foreign criticism of his own literature or to neglect to obtain a fair knowledge at least of the chief European literatures, either in the originals or through translations.

In this connection it is a pleasure to refer to a paper by Mr. Edmund Gosse, entitled " The Isolation of the Anglo-Saxon Mind," which appeared a few years ago in the *Cosmopolitan* magazine. Mr. Gosse has never given better proof of his critical acumen than in this warning against the growing insularity of the British mind. He plausibly — as it seems to me, correctly — attributes much of the British ignorance and indifference with regard to what foreigners are doing in the world of letters to the rise of rampant imperialism

which has been coincident with the growth of
Mr. Kipling's popularity. As we Americans have
done a little in the imperial line ourselves, and
have developed our own "strenuous" literature,
Mr. Gosse rather logically includes us with his
own countrymen, and warns us also against the
deplorable effects of mental isolation. While admitting the force of much that he says, I cannot,
however, think that any such marked isolation
since 1895 can be found in America as he seems
to have observed in Great Britain. The growing
vogue of French and Russian novelists in transla-
tion — Balzac, Alphonse Daudet, Flaubert, Maupassant, and even Gautier among the French,
as well as Turgenev, Tolstoy, and other Russians,
have recently been made accessible to us in whole
or in part; the increasing number of scholarly and
popular books on French and German literature;
the lecture courses given at our great universities
by distinguished French scholars [1] — these facts
seem to me to indicate that the American mind is
not closing itself to foreign influences. It surely
has not closed itself to German scholarship; and

[1] Since these words were written, the country has welcomed
many foreign scholars, who were brought over in connection with
the St. Louis Exposition.

while one occasionally reads a blatantly chauvinis-
tic article or an insularly ignorant book, I suspect
that we have a right to regard ourselves as intel-
lectually a wide-awake people.

It does not follow, however, that Mr. Gosse's
warning is not worth heeding. Conceit will
speedily make any man or any nation ignorant,
and we are by no means free from conceit, whether
as individuals or as a people. We are rightly proud
of our literary achievements, especially of those of
the entire race of which we have come to be a
most important branch; but this should not blind
us to the fact that there are other Teutonic peoples
with literatures worthy of study, nor to the equally
important fact that there is a very great body of
Romance literature well worthy of vying with our
own and supplementing it admirably. Yet when
I assert, as I am frequently forced in fairness to do,
that in my judgment the French literature of the
nineteenth century is perhaps, if not probably, superior to that produced in Great Britain during the
same period, it is always easy for me to perceive
that in nine cases out of ten the fact that such may
possibly be the case has not before dawned upon
any of the persons doing me the honor to listen to
me. This is but to say that it rarely occurs to

us to think that we have not a monopoly of literary
as well as of all the other virtues, whereas we not
only have no monopoly of the virtues, we have not
even a monopoly of the vices, other races pushing
us very closely in conceit, in ignorance, and in
their concomitant bellicosity. But surely conceit,
ignorance, and bellicosity are things to be avoided
by the attainment of a cosmopolitan outlook upon
literature and life. If, as some persons inform us,
the instinct of racial self-preservation is opposed
to cosmopolitanism, so much the worse for the
racial instinct. Humanity as a whole, is greater
than any of its parts, and a world-wide extension
of the highest ideals has been the goal of religion and art and literature and science since' man
began his arduous, upward march of progress. It
is impossible to believe that this goal will ever be
really lost sight of or that it can be achieved by
any one race, particularly by any race that relies
on mental inbreeding for its progeny of ideas, or
that depends on its muscles to do the work of its
brains. Mr. Gosse enforces his warning by a
homely story of a young Londoner who was
brought almost to his grave by a never-varied diet
of mutton chops. It would be quite possible for
a nation to be brought to an intellectual grave, or

at least to a stagnation like that to be observed in China, if, as is most improbable at this stage of the history of Western Christendom, it were, for any long time, to narrow its mental diet to the works of its own authors, and especially to the works of its own contemporary writers.

But although no great modern nation is in such a state of mental isolation, or is likely to reach it, there are always millions of persons in every generation who, often through no fault of their own, suffer from such isolation. Many teachers, writers, and scholars suffer from it badly. But surely our ideal literary student should not. In addition to endeavoring to combine in his work of self-culture the methods employed both by the professional student and by the literary amateur, he should always aim to look at every problem that confronts him from the cosmopolitan point of view, a point of view not to be attained without labor or without cordial sympathy with the best spirits of other nations. For example, it would seem very undesirable, for men aiming at ideal culture to educate themselves without the least reference to the work of Count Tolstoy or with an explosive wrath against it. Yet not a few persons place themselves in the one category or in the other. National and individual isolation in literature is just as much to be shunned as the mechanical methods of the professional student and the desultoriness of the amateur.

I am well aware, in conclusion, that all that I have said may be rightly pronounced extremely general, and, in so far, more or less common-place, inadequate, and difficult of application. But it must be remembered that literature, holding as it does by the ideal, is, like the ideal, always eluding us. No one has ever succeeded in satis-factorily defining literature, much less in telling us exactly how best to appreciate and study it. In fact, if one could teach literature with the precision with which one can teach mathematics, would the fascinating study be itself? Would it not lose much of its fascination?

But apart from the comparative impossibility of laying down hard-and-fast, concrete methods of studying literature to advantage, it should be remembered, I think, that a statement of sound general principles is often of great positive utility in furnishing us with a proper point of departure for our own studies and investigations. It is in their statement of general principles that the great

critics are as a rule most illuminating and instruc-
tive.   For this reason the "Poetics" of Aristotle,
as Mr. Courthope has shown us in his admirable
volume entitled "Life in Poetry, Law in Taste,"
is of as much value to us as it was to that philosopher's contemporaries, and of greater value than
it was to critics of two centuries ago, because the
latter emphasized and misapprehended minor and
special statements, whereas we emphasize rather
Aristotle's profound generalizations.   For this
reason, too, I venture to think, certain essays of
Matthew Arnold's — for example, that on "The
Study of Poetry" prefixed to Ward's "English
Poets" — will mean more to posterity than many
a more brilliant essay of his contemporary,
James Russell Lowell.   It is, I repeat, most
important to obtain a safe point of departure
from sound generalizations.   It is like having the
union station in a town we are leaving pointed
out to us.   We may take the wrong train after
we enter the station; but if we go wandering
about the town, we shall get no train at all.

I am not sure, of course, that the generalizations I have given are worthy of confidence, but
experience teaches me to think that they are.
I believe that the reason why men and women

are turning more and more to literary studies is that they find in them the readiest means of access to the ideal. I believe that those students who, like myself, make literature a profession are constantly in danger of mistaking the letter of their pursuit for its spirit, and of prosecuting mechanically a study that should engage the highest faculties of mind and heart and soul. Hence I am sure that the professional student will find it profitable always to bear in mind the aims and methods of the lovers of literature whom, for convenience, we call amateurs. On the other hand, I am convinced that, while the aims of many amateurs are high, their methods of approaching literature are often narrow, inconsistent, unintelligent, and their purposes too self-centred. They may, therefore, profit greatly by following the guidance of competent critics and teachers — in other words, by acknowledging some authority in matters of taste besides their own sweet wills. In short, I give my allegiance neither to an aristocracy of letters, a so-called class of cultured Mandarins in whom all learning resides, nor to a democracy of letters, in which every man's judgment is as good as his neighbor's, but to a constitutional republic of letters like the United States in politics — a republic in which there are both aristocratic and democratic classes or estates, which can flourish only through mutual intelligence and coöperation and through cultivating the friendliest international relations. This means that we need a critic to do for students of British and American literature what Burke has done for students of British and American politics. After we get him, we may perhaps look forward to the time when a great modern Aristotle shall apply the critical method to the chaos of knowable things, and give the world a "Synthetic Philosophy" that shall surpass even the great structure of Herbert Spencer. In the meanwhile, we whose functions and aspirations are much humbler may labor while we wait, may somewhat lighten his labors, and may prepare men and women to appreciate them. For to prepare men and women to study literature is really to prepare them to appreciate the highest mental and moral achievements.

IV

CRITICISM AND FAITH

[The substance of two short papers contributed to *The Churchman*, October 2, 1897, and February 12, 1898.]

IV

CRITICISM AND FAITH

I

I HAVE just been re-reading one of the most
subtle of M. Jules Lemaître's charming char-
acterizations of his contemporaries — I mean
the four pages that he devoted some years ago
to M. Ferdinand Brunetière in the collection of
sketches entitled "Figurines." As the reading
world has long known, M. Lemaître and M. Brunetière are as far apart as the poles in their critical methods and ideals. Each is a master in his
way, each has always been conscious of his
rival's influence and power; hence every thrust
and parry of the duel they have waged has its
interest for the spectator. In that particular stage
of the encounter to which I referred above, M.
Lemaître gave a thrust so clever, so unexpected
that he might well have been pardoned for
deeming it a home thrust indeed. I myself

may perhaps be pardoned for trying to give
an English equivalent of it: —

"One must have seen at times, in some con-
vent when the middle age was at its zenith, a
theologian-monk, ardent in controversy, orthodox, but rash in his dialectic to the point of
making one tremble, austere, secretive, never
giving a glimpse of his heart or of his sensations, hard in aspect and a stranger to every
pleasure. . . . One morning his brothers found
him hanged in his cell, beneath his large cruci-
fix. What had taken place? A drama of
metaphysical speculations ending in despair?
a drama of mortal ennui? or something still less
to be suspected?

"My pleasantry is not of a gay kind, and it
is horribly romantic. But M. Brunetière makes
me think, in spite of myself, of a theologian
damned."

Now I do not propose to discuss this duel
in detail, but simply wish to ask why M.
Lemaître took the trouble to deliver this particular thrust. Perhaps he acted on the principle that your own strongest point is likely to
be your adversary's weakest. This may be a
bad principle, but Lemaître plainly believed that

his own strength consisted in an utter independence of all critical standards save those of individual preference, and that Brunetière's weakness lay in his distrust of himself and in his acquiescence in established opinions and judgments. Be this as it may, there is surely food for reflection for us in the position taken by the impressionist critic.

Are critical standards a hindrance or a help? or, in other words, Can a man in literature, any more than in life, dispense with faith in something higher than himself? Yes, M. Lemaître appeared to say; no, M. Brunetière would doubtless have replied. And yet the former critic, in the essay from which I have quoted, assured us that his rival was pessimistic to the core — that therefore he was profoundly melancholy and that to give himself the solace of work, he labored indefatigably "to defend principles and institutions" in which he did not "believe."

But this is a curious rôle for a pessimist to play — especially when he is credited with being sincere. Is it fair to call a man a pessimist when his whole life has been a consistent struggle for principles which, he claims, possess validity through the fact that they are based on something

higher than his own belief in them — to wit, on the
credence accorded them by generation upon generation of thinking men? Did not Lemaître
change rapiers in the contest, and was he able to
handle his adversary's effectively? Was he not
himself the pessimist in spite of his jaunty mien
and his alluring smile? The man who frankly
confesses his disbelief in the power of his fellows
to find standards of right thinking in matters of
art is just as truly a pessimist as the man who
can discover no standards of conduct, no rules of
life based on faith in God and fellow-men. How
shall we write or live effectively or consistently if
we have not a pattern, an example, to guide us?
We cannot know what we may safely enjoy in
art unless we have standards of judgment and
taste, any more than we can know what drugs are
wholesome unless we have standards of experience.
The coarse novel, the obscene picture, may be like
the brilliantly colored drug, attractive to the eye,
but deadly to the taste. Now we should surely
call a man who consistently flouted the lessons of
experience either a fool or a pessimist *à outrance;*
but experience applies not merely to the physical
and moral spheres, but to the artistic as well. To
be seduced by the blue depths of the lake, by the

red lights of the bar-room, by the yellow covers of the foul novel — are kindred catastrophes in a sense. All sooner or later result in death of one sort or another, and all proceed, either from ignorance or thoughtlessness — cases we are not here considering — or from the wilful setting up of one's own judgment against the experience of the race. Self-assertion is a basis if not the chief basis of pessimism, and faith is the main basis of optimism, nor do all M. Lemaître's subtle powers of fence save him from falling at last before the keen point of this fundamental truth.

M. Brunetière may have many points in common with the mediæval monk of M. Lemaître's imagination. His recent turning to Roman Catholicism seems to show this. He has faith in ideals and standards, and he believes that it is his duty to try to win the world to these; but he has not shut himself up in a cell, and so long as he follows 'the precepts of the gospel of work, he is not likely to hang himself. If any such fate could legitimately have been predicted ten years ago as in store for either of the rivals, it was for M. Lemaître himself. It might have been imagined that, jaded with a multiplicity of sensations leading no whither, he would some day realize that life had no charms left, and that some one would be impelled to draw a companion picture representing him as a sated Epicurean lying dead and deserted amid the paraphernalia of a soulless luxury. Fortunately, neither rival has yet perished either by his own or by the other's hand, and the world has had so many larger and more important contests to witness that it has almost forgotten their various passages at arms. Some of us have not forgotten, however, the sides on which they fought, nor are we disconcerted in having M. Brunetière of late sally forth in defence of authority in another garb against other foes. We still remember some of the lessons we learned from him. We still believe that here in this new land of half-formed ideals we can by no means afford to dissociate art from conduct, that in both we have continual need of standards—that is, of faith in the true, the beautiful, and the good, not as they merely seem to be such to us, but as they always have existed and always will exist beyond and above ourselves within the bosom of God.

II

That faith of some sort is as necessary to the critic as it is to the man who wishes to lead a good

life and do a good work in this perplexing world
is a point not only, I hope, brought out by the com-
ments made above, but also, it would seem, involved in what was said in a former paper about
the propriety of laying emphasis upon the value of
popular judgment in literary and artistic matters.
Yet I fancy that most persons, if they were to
think about the matter at all, would opine at first
blush that good criticism is much more an affair
of scepticism than one of faith.

Perhaps one reason why so many people, forgetting that comparatively sterile periods seem to
be needed in order to enable creative forces to
gather strength, regret the fact that the period in
which we live is on the whole one of criticism
rather than of consummate literary creation, is to
be found in the close affiliation scepticism seems
to have with criticism, scepticism being naturally
repellent to normally healthy minds. There is
no inherent reason why criticism should be pre-
dominantly sceptical in character, but it often is so,
and the public seems generally to assume that it
will be so. Throughout the nineteenth century it
was the sceptical side of criticism that forced itself
upon public attention, mainly because it exhibited
piquant and sensational characteristics. There is

a plain element of the sensational in the mainte-
nance of the Baconian authorship of the Shaksper-
ian plays, which is not entirely lacking in the
criticism that makes Homer a myth and Captain
John Smith a mere braggadocio.   One can be
much more piquant when one is combating a
theory or an opinion universally held to be true,
than when one is saying for the thousandth time
what one is expected to say.

Of late there has seemed, however, to be a feeling among all classes of critics that the sceptical
spirit has led them too far, and perhaps it is not
too much to say that a reaction is slowly setting in
which will tend to restore to modern criticism
some of the popular respect it has lost.   The
late Mr. Fiske's defence of the veracity of Captain
John Smith is an example in point, because it was
based on the strictly scientific desire to find an
explanation for something posited as true, rather
than on the purely sceptical desire to sweep
away something that did not square with normal
experience.   Still more striking, perhaps, is the
attitude of a few critics toward Defoe, whose
character cannot be completely rehabilitated but
whose positive statements no sensible man is likely
to dismiss jauntily as the utterances of " the great-

est liar that ever lived," now that Mr. G. A. Aitken
has clearly proved that all the details given in the
famous ghost story of " Mrs. Veal" were obtained
by Defoe in precisely the way that would be
employed by a modern reporter sent to investigate a matter interesting to the public.

This anti-sceptical tendency, which may be
observed throughout the world of thought, will
be of great importance in literary and artistic
criticism if it is allowed free play. The popular
standing of an author or an artist of established
reputation is the posited fact, and truly scientific
criticism will endeavor to account for this reputation, to maintain it, and even to unfold it, rather
than to assert that modern taste finds little to
enjoy in what has pleased our ancestors. It is
much easier to decry and endeavor to dethrone,
than it is to serve loyally in matters of criticism.
If we succeed in showing that some long-popular
author is after all really of no great consequence ;
if we prove that a forgotten writer is in fact deserv-
ing of immortal bays, we naturally expect that we
shall come in for more glory than we should if we
were to choose the less ambitious part of praising,
in our turn, what has long been regarded as a just
subject of praise.

This is but to say that if there is a reaction
against sceptical criticism, it will make itself felt
in matters literary and artistic by encouraging
academic at the expense of impressionist criticism.
The impressionist is in most cases sceptical of the
judgments of others, because he is too prone to over-
value his own.   But the desire to pass unique judgments of one's own leads at once to the desire to
sweep away that which is posited about authors
and books, painters and pictures, and the sweep-
ing away of posited judgments produces as disastrous effects in literary criticism as the more
obvious but closely related sceptical methods of
treatment produce in historical studies.

It is almost needless to say, in conclusion, that
I do not wish to be accused of heralding a return
of the old, unquestioning spirit of acceptance of
all that antiquity has handed down to us.   Modern
science has done its work too thoroughly for such
a spirit to be again dominant among cultivated
people, or for any sane man to wish that it should
become dominant.   My desire is simply to point
out the fact that if the purely sceptical spirit in
criticism continues to be held in check, sounder
methods of study will be applied to literature and
the arts, the judgments of past generations will be

treated with respect and modified only when necessary, and academic criticism will receive its due recognition. There will be fewer surprises in store for the readers of our magazines, who will not be confronted each month with some new candidate for fame, but the great masters will receive more and more adequate comprehension and applause.

V

LITERATURE AND SCIENCE

[Delivered before the Phi Beta Kappa of Lehigh University, June, 1904.]

V

LITERATURE AND SCIENCE

It is very commonly assumed that there is a necessary antagonism of ends and methods between those who devote themselves to scientific pursuits and those who occupy themselves with any of the fine arts, whether as a calling or as a pastime. That this antagonism is often visible enough will scarcely be denied — certainly not by any one who has ever sat in a college faculty. That it is necessary is something I have not been able to perceive during the nearly twenty years of my academic experience. I have never looked upon my scientific associates as rivals to be fought with and circumvented, and I have striven, while maintaining my own devotion to literature, to give them no occasion to view me in such a sinister light. Perhaps this fact will serve as an excuse for my rashness in attempting to discuss afresh the very large and timeworn subject of the relations of science and literature, especially

III

as constituent parts of that indefinite something denominated culture.

In such a discussion the first step, obviously, is to try to define the terms employed. Here, however, we encounter an initial difficulty which will prove insuperable if we are strenuous in maintaining our rights. Scientists may have defined science in a manner satisfactory to themselves, but I am very sure that no literary man's definition of literature has ever long satisfied any other literary man. It goes without saying that no man of letters (if only for shame's sake) would allow a scientist to define literature for him. Hence, if we insist upon definitions, this discussion may as well be adjourned indefinitely.

There is, however, another plane than that of accepted definitions, upon which the scientist and the literary man may meet for discussion. It is the Socratic plane — the plane of consecutive questions and answers, without, however, the trap-door through which Socrates's opponents used to disappear in an undignified manner.

Let each ask himself what he is about, what his primary concern is as scientist or man of letters respectively. The scientist will probably reply that he is striving to advance the bounds of systematic human knowledge. The historian, the biographer, or the critic might conceivably make this answer also; but, if a true man of letters, he would at once add something to the effect that he was at the same time and with equal, or at least considerable zeal, striving to increase the sum of human pleasure. The scientist might rejoin that such was his purpose as well, and he might easily show how the discoveries of science have redounded to human happiness. But when the two had threshed their meanings out, it would probably appear that the end of giving pleasure to others was only a subsidiary one with the scientist, whereas it was a primary and vital one with the literary historian, biographer, or critic. I may illustrate the point I am trying to bring out, by saying that the historian who confessed that he had but one primary aim, viz., to add to the sum of human knowledge about a particular period of a nation's history, would at once be disowned by men of letters. If the scientists would not receive him on account of the fact that he could not apply absolutely rigid tests to determine the credibility of the results of his work, the rejected individual would have to flock with the economists, the students of politics, law, and similar subjects — that is, with what we may call the semi-scientists, among whom he could doubtless make himself comfortable.

But historians, biographers, and critics who do not regard the extension of the bounds of systematized knowledge as their sole primary aim, and are hence entitled to call themselves men of letters, are generally regarded, after all, as servants or suspected aliens within the realm of literature. Some of them actually subscribe to their own inferiority to a minor poet or a third-rate novelist; but this will probably not be for long, since minor poets and third-rate novelists are increasing with such rapidity under our tolerant laws that the day may be not far distant when writing poems and novels will be almost as commonplace a domestic phenomenon as china painting and embroidering now are. We are not concerned, however, with the ranking of authors or with the loss of distinction which some of them may incur, if books continue to be manufactured and sold like shoes. What we wish to know is how a truly great poet or novelist would answer our question as to the primary purpose for which he writes.

Whatever form his answer might take, it is almost inconceivable, I think, that it should be

that of the scientist,—to extend the bounds of systematized knowledge. The great creative writers
do extend the bounds of knowledge very materi-
ally in certain ways ; but their ways are not those
of the scientist, the knowledge they furnish is
rarcly of the kind he deals with, — though Tennyson, I believe, did give, or else might have given,
a fact or two to the botanist, — and the extension
of the bounds of knowledge is scarcely, if at all,
in their thoughts when they are in the act of
composing. As for the lesser creative writers, —
especially in these days of art for art's sake, — it
is needless to say that they would disclaim any
intention of trying to extend the bounds of human
knowledge. Indeed, how could many of them
make such a claim without turning scarlet ?

But our questioning has not carried us very far.
Scientists and semi-scientists, from the greatest
to the least, have one clear, common end in view.
This end is shared partly only by some kinds
of writers, while, if writers as a class have one
clear, common end in view, it is certainly not that
of the scientists. Given that most normal of human characteristics, — the desire to pursue one's
own end unimpeded, to make it triumph over the
end another is pursuing, to attract other adherents

to it, — why should we not suppose that scientists and men of letters will maintain more or less antagonistic relations till time is no more ? What wonder is it that the present poet laureate should complain that in this age of science there is a marked decrease of interest in the higher forms of poetry ? What wonder is it that history and biography, categories of literature the spirit of which is least alien to that of science, should daily be gaining favor, as we are told, with serious readers ? What wonder, finally, that in our schools, colleges, and universities, scientific and semi-scientific studies have not only been winning their rightful place in the curriculum, but have taken on an aggressive attitude that threatens the very existence of certain more or less literary courses, particularly those in Greek and Latin, without which the study of literature in the vernacular can be prosecuted only in a halting and incomplete manner ?

That the day will ever come when no professor of physics will be impelled to ask, as one did the other day in New York, why boys would not be better employed in studying the motions of the planets than in learning the names of obscure and obscene heathen divinities, I hesitate to affirm.

Such a protesting professor will always have Plato for something of a prototype and a long line of utilitarians for successors. Much less do I dare to affirm that the day will ever come in which artists and men of letters, whenever they can indulge their prejudices in safety, will cease to display ignorance and bad temper at the mention of science. But I should also and to an equal degree be disinclined to asseverate that class hatred will cease short of some sort of a millennium, or that nations will in any calculable future refrain from settling certain classes of disputes by the barbaric means of war ; yet I am willing to maintain that class hatred and wars between nations are unnecessary evils, on the supposition that man is a free agent capable of distinguishing and choosing the better from the worse.   In other words, the fact that something will probably long continue to exist should not deter us from questioning whether it ought to exist — should not disincline us to ask,

> " Can such things be,
> And overcome us like a summer's cloud,
> Without our special wonder ? "

Now I am never made aware of the antagonisms that exist among men to whom the things

of the mind are of primary concern, without a very
special wonder.   Scientists and artists, men of
letters and scholars, may find it difficult to discover a clear purpose held in common; but one
and all, in accomplishing their respective tasks,
they are envisaging this mysterious universe of
which they are insignificant parts.   One and all
they stand in the presence of an Awful Reality,
who to the poet may be

> "God — the mighty source
> Of all things — the stupendous force
>   On which all strength depends;
> From whose right arm, beneath whose eyes,
> All period, power, and enterprise
>   Commences, reigns, and ends — "

or who to the philosopher may be that "insoluble
enigma," which man "evermore perceives to be
an insoluble enigma."   In such a presence how
are human antagonisms possible?   How, except
on the supposition that the clear, common end
which we found for the scientists and ceased to
inquire for in the case of the men of letters, is
not, after all, the ultimate end for either?   If the
final end of science and the final end of literature
and every other art be not to envisage " steadily "
and "whole," as best may be, this mysterious

universe and to bring the minds and souls of
scientists and artists and writers and of all who
profit from their labors most completely and be-
comingly into the presence of the Awful Reality,
are science and art and literature fully compre-
hended by their votaries?

It is most necessary at this point to avoid all
temptation or inclination to drop into cant — that
besetting weakness of Anglo-Saxons. It is so
easy to talk about wonder and awe without feeling them, so easy to miss the solid and necessary facts of life while groping about in the
spacious and nebulous region of ideas. Yet can
the scientific mind that stops short in its probing,
that does not question until it encounters the inscrutable mystery of the universe, be regarded as
fulfilling its functions properly and completely, or
can the creative faculty of the artist that does not
impinge upon the same inscrutable mystery be
looked on as worthy of special admiration? Did
not Newton and Darwin, Shakspere and Milton,
however different the paths they blazed through
the forests of nature and life, emerge upon the
shore of the same infinite ocean? And unless we
also, following paths already cut or making them
for ourselves, finally get a glimpse of

" that immortal ſea
Which brought us hither,"

will not our last state be that of wanderers lost in
tangled and impenetrable woods ? We may make a
circle with our steps and fancy we are progressing,
or we may lie down in a spot which in our hallu-
cination we take to be our true goal; yet, if we
do these things, shall we be any the less pitiable
because we are complacent? But do those who
emerge on the shore of the infinite sea strive to
drown with their objurgations and rival clamors
the rhythmical plash of its waves ? Or is it
sensible for wanderers in a forest to pelt one
another with missiles, when their paths happen
to cross or to lie side by side ?

But it may be urged that, if all this is not cant,
it is very figurative and far from being clear-cut
and definitive.   Such an objection has force,
although it should be remembered that many
high forms of truth are only with great difficulty, if at all, to be expressed in terms of the
concrete and definite. I will confess further that
in one important particular my figure breaks down.
He who has once emerged upon the shore of the
infinite ocean becomes endowed with a power
never granted to toilers through actual and tan-

gible forests. He may renew his toils and wan-
derings in other parts of the thickets of life and
nature, and yet always have the power, not
merely of remembering the sight of the great
ocean, but of transporting himself at any moment
to its margin. To put it differently, the true scientist and the true artist or man of letters, having
once grasped firmly the idea that his ultimate purpose is to help on man's interpretation of the universe in its marvellous entirety, never lets go that
idea, even when he is absorbed in a delicate piece
of investigation, or in painting a miniature, or in
polishing a sonnet. Adequately to express this
great truth in figurative terms of concrete human
action will be, I think, impossible so long as a man
is unable to be in two places at the same time. It
is none the less certain, however, that the really
successful creative mind, whether in science or in
art, moves simultaneously in the two spheres of the
finite and the infinite, and that this is not a metaphysical impossibility, since the larger sphere includes the lesser.

Perhaps it is now sufficiently plain, not only
why opposition between scientists and men of
letters is not necessary, but also why they should
regard themselves as brothers ever ready to lend a

helping hand to one another. In many particulars the subject-matters with which they deal respectively, the methods they apply, the proximate ends and purposes they have in view, are so distinct that it is no wonder that at first thought occasions for misunderstanding, if not of strife, present themselves. But in the final analysis their main end is a common one, however different the means by which it is to be accomplished. That end, as we have seen, is the more complete interpretation of the universe in its entirety, and the chief reason why contentions arise between the two classes of interpreters is that neither fully and continually realizes that the universe is in itself, for the purposes of ultimate interpretation, an indissoluble entity. We, being finite and a part of it, portion it out into mechanical and metaphysical segments and devote ourselves to the study and understanding of one or more of these purely relative and often purely ideal divisions, forgetting the while that we are dealing only with the perceptions of our senses and the creations of our intellectual and imaginative faculties, and not with that indissoluble entity, the interpretation or partial interpretation of which, though it be the mystery of mysteries, is also the desire of desires and the dream of dreams of the aspiring soul of man. It is our doom, of course, since we are finite, never to interpret the universe completely, and it is also our doom to move forward only by slow, almost imperceptible degrees toward such a partial interpretation of it as will not seem unworthy of intelligent beings. Hence there should be no repining at the necessity we are under of dealing with perceived or imagined segments instead of with the transcendant whole. Yet, while in our finiteness we are so constituted that we can take pleasure in dealing with the parts we perceive and create, in our infinite aspirations we are dwarfed and emasculated if we do not keep always before us the entire universe, material and spiritual, — in other words, the ultimate phenomenon.

But the moment we grasp the idea that the mind's problem of problems is to square itself with the universe, it becomes apparent that the larger and more comprehensive the mind can be made, the wider view it will take of the universe and the nearer it will come to the desiderated interpretation. Civilization is but another name for this endlessly repeated process of squaring the mind of the race with the universe. Yet we surely do not make the mind larger and more comprehensive if we insist that it shall deal in the main only with sense-perceptions or in the main only with ideas, or if we insist that it shall employ only one set of methods with which to envisage the universe. Nor do we display much acumen, if in the presence of an indissoluble phenomenon, we spend our time in wrangling over the fruitless question as to which of two or more sets of relative phenomena may fairly be said to be of greater or greatest importance. I may be preternaturally dull, but I must frankly confess that I have never been able to see how science can be more important than art or art than science. Both are indispensable to any interpretation of the universe, if only for the reason that the one answers chiefly to the intellectual, the other chiefly to the emotional nature of man, the interpreter. The universe in which we live is one of passions as well as of stars, of stages of thought as well as of geological strata, of sighs of love and sorrow as well as of cataclysmal forces. Perhaps on "this dim spot which men call earth" the steam-engine has made a deeper impression than the sonnet, but the one is, in the last analysis, no less wonderful than the other, and to leave either out of account in an attempted interpretation of the universe would be fatal. Yet how often do we see the poet and the mechanical engineer bound together by the ties of intelligent sympathy? How often does a professor of literature urge his students to give a fair amount of their time to his colleague who lectures on chemistry, and how often does the latter return the courtesy? But such sympathies and such courtesies should not be rare among men whose common concern is with the wonders of the universe.

If, then, there is one idea that ought to emerge more prominently and frequently than any other in a discussion of the relations of science and literature, — or science and art, if you will, for literature in this connection must be conceived as an art, — it is the idea of catholicity. Man, the interpreter, is a whole, and the universe which he must strive to interpret, if he is not to live in it as a mere animal, is a whole also. The whole interpreter must take a whole view of the whole phenomenon — that is to say, man, to be worthy of his high attributes, must be catholic in his aims and methods, especially when he is bringing his powers to bear on subjects of vast importance to his spiritual, mental, and bodily welfare. He does injustice to himself when he fancies that he can pursue and capture Truth without at the same time pursuing and capturing her sister Beauty. Indeed, man must not, like Apollo, pursue a single nymph — he must pursue Three Graces whose names are Truth, Beauty, and Goodness. If he pursues a sole and single object, no matter how desirable, he must expect a metamorphosis and a frustration. Instead of the nymph the god grasped a bough of laurel, from the leaves of which he wove a garland for his brow. So the scientist pursuing Truth alone may grasp new and important facts, the poet pursuing Beauty alone may snatch exquisite harmonies and images, and both may gain plaudits that will partly repay them for their endeavors; but neither will achieve the true object of his pursuit, for facts are not Truth nor are exquisite harmonies and images Beauty, any more than the shapely laurel was the flying nymph. This is old doctrine, and never better expressed than by Keats when he wrote

"'Beauty is Truth, Truth Beauty' — this is all
Ye know on earth and all ye need to know."

Add the third member of the trinity, Goodness, and we have the Golden Rule transferred from the sphere of conduct to that of thought and emotion. But it is only the catholic man who can come near to living up to the Golden Rule.

What now should be the practical outcome of the adoption of a catholic attitude toward the claims of science and art — especially literature — as constituent parts in human education or culture? In the first place, it would seem that every catholic-minded man should rejoice in all the triumphs of science and in all the achievements of art; that jealousy should be banished, save that commendable jealousy for the honor of one's chosen pursuit; that the complete democratic equality of all the arts and sciences should be proclaimed throughout the thinking and the reading world. The last statement does not mean, of course, that there should be no differences of prestige among the arts and sciences, any more than the assertion of democratic equality in the sphere of politics means that descent from a long line of honorable ancestors should carry no weight in a normally constituted community. You can no more put history out of doors with a fork than you can expel nature with the same instrument. The poet Horace, whose words I have just used, derives much of his prestige from the fact that his

poems have been handed down for nearly two
thousand years; but if he were writing to-day, he
would enjoy, rightly or wrongly, a sort of prestige
over many other writers and over certain classes
of scientific investigators merely because he would
come before the public crowned with the venerable
title of poet. The mineralogist, on the other hand,
in spite of the truth and beauty of the systems of
crystallography he expounds, must long expect to
have his books read and his classes attended, save
in rare cases, only by a few persons of special
endowments and proclivities. But the mineralogist
has his compensations, and he can take his stand
by the side of the poet upon the margin of the
infinite sea. He, too, is helping man to interpret
the universe.

Another consequence of the adoption of a catholic attitude toward the respective claims of science
and literature in education ought to be a cessation of
wrangling among those who frame the curriculums
of our schools and colleges. Discussion as to the
relative amounts of each to be allowed, as to the
divisions of students to be effected according to
their respective aptitudes, as to relative value in
mental training, and similar subjects must continue, indeed, for many a day to come; and if

my colleagues of the so-called humane studies persist in holding their inherited, not personally achieved, ground in such a Bourbon-like fashion, I fear that my colleagues of the natural sciences will for a long time be justified in banding together to resist ultraconservatism by radical aggression. But wrangling is at no time necessary, and it is to be hoped that the outcome of every contest between extreme conservatism and irritated radicalism will be true progress. And if reason and catholicity prevail, as they doubtless will in the long run, the questions at issue will be answered by a sound pedagogy, which must be based upon educational history in its broadest sense and experimental psychology. When that day comes, there will be no "college fetich" to give offence and, let us hope, no denouncers of it to give still greater offence by their denunciations. Yet I suspect that in that blessed time Greek, the most beautiful of languages, preserved in the most perfect of literatures, will still be taught, even in those universities in which for good and sufficient reasons the chief emphasis is laid upon science.

A third consequence of the adoption of a catholic attitude seems to be more important still. The scientist will gain inspiration and concrete help in greater abundance from the man of letters and the artist, and the man of letters and the artist will in turn gain inspiration and help from the scientist. Precisely what benefits will flow to the scientist I am not specially competent to say; but he cannot fail to be a better scientist if he becomes a better man, and a better man he is sure to be if he lives in charity with his fellow-interpreters of the universe and if he submits his emotional nature to the charms of art and literature. Some of the aberrations of literary taste displayed by Herbert Spencer have recently been subjected to comment, and capital has been so frequently made of Darwin's confession with regard to the starving of his æsthetic faculties, that one hesitates to mention it, especially if one belongs to the literary class that has used it as a text for numerous sermons. Still, with no intention of preaching, I may say that, whenever a full, catholic understanding is arrived at between the votaries of science and those of literature, it is altogether likely that scientists will be less self-centred than they now are, more alive to the æsthetic appeal made by the world whose material phenomena it is their chief concern to investigate, more interested in human life with its mysterious and complex forces, and, finally, more willing to admit that the phenomena we vaguely denominate spiritual are not only worthy of the fullest scientific investigation, but are also often set in relief and thus made amenable to study by the subtle insight and the plastic genius of the artist and the writer. In other words, the day will surely come when creative genius in art and letters will not be merely a source of innocuous and unimportant pleasure to some scientists, or an object of study with a particular branch of them, to wit, the alienists. Yet, as I speak, I realize that I am doing the scientific mind an injustice in implying that it does not often take seriously the serious art of the world. John Stuart Mill was not a born scientist, but his was preëminently a scientific mind, and it was more receptive of the early poetry of Robert Browning than were the minds of nine out of ten professed critics in the England of the thirties and the forties.

With regard to the inspiration and concrete help to be gained by men of letters from the adoption of a catholic attitude toward scientific interpreters of the universe, I can perhaps speak a little more definitely. Creative literature, certainly in its objective forms, such as the epic, the drama, the novel, rests primarily upon observation of human and, to a less extent, of external nature. Even in its subjective forms, such as the lyric poem, literature rests upon a certain amount of self-observation or introspection, although the writer may be unconscious of the fact when he is in the fervor of actual creation. But observation is one of the two foundation stones upon which the whole structure of science has been reared. The other foundation stone of science is experiment, which is also indispensable, not merely to every man of letters who wishes to test his powers, but also to literature, if it is to be a thing of growth and adaptation to human needs. That the experimental tests of the scientist are vastly different from those of the man of letters is a statement that needs scarcely to be made; but it is equally obvious that the results of every writer's observation are continually being tested both by himself and by his critics and readers. Constant recognition of the latter fact and sympathy with the mental attitude of cautious pursuit of accuracy characteristic of the scientist cannot but be beneficial to the writer by increasing his sense of responsibility and by reminding him of the impermanence, not to say the impertinence, of slipshod work.

But the self-consciousness which is necessary
to the scientific investigator, even if it vitiates
his work to a degree determinable by the "personal equation," is often more or less of a draw-
back to the writer; hence experiment is of far
less significance to him than observation. Even
the wildest romancer is more dependent upon
observation of the facts of life than would appear at first thought; and the great creative
writer, whether in prose or in verse, is absolutely dependent upon it. The more accurate
his observation, and in many cases the more
minute, the more authentic his genius. Balzac
described the houses of Saumur as minutely
almost as a botanist describes a plant.
Thackeray, writing in his last years a romance of England at the end of the eighteenth century, left behind him topographical
and biographical notes so numerous and so
careful that it is easy to judge in the main
the course the unfinished story of "Denis
Duval" would have followed. Shakspere has
left us no manuscript notes of the observations
which enabled him to develop an Italian story
or an old chronicle play or a tragedy of blood
into a consummate dramatic masterpiece; but

if he did not take his notes on paper or on a tablet of the kind he speaks of in his "Sonnets," he took them in his capacious and retentive mind. In literature, however, observation deals not alone with the external and the material; it is concerned with thoughts as well as with actions, with ideas as well as with facts. Here is where literary observation differs from most varieties of scientific observation, and here is precisely where, in my judgment, the man of letters has most to learn from his fellow-interpreter of the universe. Having to observe and explain the actions of men, the creative writer is ever laboring under the temptation to square the facts of life with theories of life and the universe which he has accepted upon hearsay or through inherited prejudices. He is rarely as honest and thorough in his observation or study of ideas as he is in his observation of individuals and types. For example, Maupassant could sketch a Norman peasant to the life, but he gave little evidence of having studied with equal fidelity the social system that has made that rural brute a possibility. In other words, no writer, not even a Shakspere or a Balzac, appears to me comparable with a scientist in the impartiality and thoroughness of his observation. Should he aim to be or should we wish him to be? Is it not enough that his observation be sufficiently accurate to give us the pleasures that accompany æsthetic illusion? I am quite sure that many persons would answer these questions in the affirmative, but I cannot. For me the great writer must be the great interpreter of life, and to be such he must see it steadily and see it whole, as Matthew Arnold said Sophocles did. I hold implicitly and unwaveringly to Keats's apothegm, " Beauty is Truth, Truth Beauty," and I perceive nothing but æsthetic loss when a fragment of necessary truth escapes the artist's hand. Unnecessary truth is, to be sure, a phrase that means more to an artist than to a scientist or to an ultra-realistic novelist. We accept readily a Hamlet stout and short of breath, but we should reject a Hamlet with a nose as large as Cyrano's. In our rejection, however, we should be really relying upon accurate and more or less scientific observation, which teaches us that to centre attention upon a physical characteristic is to obscure to some extent those spiritual and mental characteristics which are the mainsprings of dramatic action. It may be safely affirmed, nevertheless, that in the realm of ideas the phrase "unnecessary truth" has far less meaning to the writer than it has in the realm of facts. His theories of life, his ideas about man and his environment, should be thought out to the last point of analysis, and should be squared with every observation it has been within his power to make. When he accepts a theory of politics, a system of religion, a social order, without accurate observation and investigation, he does so at his peril. He may be excused for not being ahead of his generation, but unless he possesses compensating merits, he runs the risk of being valued solely as an exponent of his epoch; in other words, as possessing historical importance merely. Even Shakspere has suffered somewhat from the fact that the spirit of Tudor absolutism is more in evidence in his plays than that of modern democracy. Thackeray suffers as compared with Dickens because, whether the latter could draw a conventional gentleman or not, the former, with all his ability to detect the follies of individuals, undoubtedly regarded the social set in which he lived and moved rather with the partiality of an easy-going

clubman than with the impartiality of the philosophical observer of life or with the amused
tolerance of the cosmopolitan democrat. Shakspere and Thackeray, however, possessed and
exercised such wonderful powers of observation
in so many fields both of facts and of ideas
that their limitations are not merely pardoned,
but almost overlooked.   Inconsistently, enough,
we do not similarly overlook the limitations of
Milton and Byron ; but the main point is that
all these writers would have been greater still
if their observation had been still more extended
in the realm of ideas.   This is but to say that
the absolute unwillingness of the scientist to
leave a single phenomenon uninvestigated ought
to be true of the writer, within the limits set
by our fallible nature.   The boundaries between
fact and fancy should not be passed by writer
or by reader without a clear recognition of
the step taken.   When that step has been
taken in an unambiguous manner, the writer
may carry us whithersoever his imagination
leads, provided only that he obey the laws of
artistic consistency.   Within the realm of the
actual his duty to us is as clear and ineluctable
as that of the scientist — he must observe as

thoroughly and impartially as is possible, in order that he may the more completely interpret to us the universe as he sees it. Absolute honesty and absolute thoroughness of observation are the watchwords of the writer just as truly as they are those of the scientist; or, to vary the figure, both march under the same banner, — a tricolor, the stripes of which coincide with that trinity of truth, beauty, and goodness about which poets have sung and philosophers expounded since the dawn of civilization.

Time is wanting for a careful consideration of a point which will very probably occur here to many, — to wit, the bearing of these remarks upon certain forms of literature in which observation scarcely seems to play the important part it does in such works as the plays of Sophocles and the novels of Balzac. The dreamer, the symbolist, the mystic, the idealist — what have these in common with the chemist and his blowpipe? This much at least, as I have already said, — they must obey the laws of artistic consistency, or, to put it otherwise, they must apply to the universe of their fancy or imagination the observation that can alone make it coherent and harmonious. If they do not do this, and if they do not make clear the relations borne by their creations to the visible, concrete universe in which they as writers and we as readers move and have our being, they cannot be great writers, simply because they cannot be sane and honest writers. We should be uncatholic if we did not give the fullest scope to dreamers and idealists, we should hamper art without benefiting science; but we should be false to our highest duty, that of interpreting the universe, if, without protest, we allowed the dreamer to call his dreams realities, or the idealist to lure us into believing that he has actually discovered a world different from that in which our lots are cast. To talk of higher realities is to talk of nonsense. To deny the existence of determinable realities is logical, although convincing to but few; to discover transcendent realities in the shape of ideals and symbols, or of concrete phenomena that elude all observation save that of the elect, is in the last analysis immoral. When we pass the boundaries of the known and the knowable, we shall, if we be honest, furl our tricolor and unfurl another banner, whether it be a streamer of fancy or a flag bearing on its field the anchor of hope.

In illustration of these remarks, let me cite three creations of English writers, all of which

are ideal, all wonderfully poetic, but of which
two seem thoroughly sound, the third partly un-
sound. The first is "The Tempest" of Shakspere, the second, the "Comus" of Milton, the
third, the "Epipsychidion" of Shelley. "The
Tempest" is the most exquisite, just as "Comus"
is probably the purest of idealistic compositions
in the English tongue; both are the products
of noble and wholesome imaginations moving in
enchanted and enchanting regions never disturbed
by "the tread of hateful steps" or even "of some
chaste footing"; but both are wonderfully true to
the laws of truth, beauty, and goodness as we see
them work in this unenchanted and often unen-
chanting world of ours. "The Tempest" is as
fundamentally honest as "Hamlet." But the
"Epipsychidion" of Shelley, which in turn transports us to an ideal spot, although, if studied only
in the light of its marvellous lyrical intensity and
pictorial power, it must always rank among
poetic masterpieces, is not an essentially honest
and moral work because it had its source in a
false set of human relations and in mistaken ideals
of love. Shelley in writing the poem did an
injustice to his faithful wife, to the Italian girl
who inspired it, to himself, and to humanity. It

is idle to suppose that the "Epipsychidion" can be accepted as a poem divorced from its setting in the facts of Shelley's life. The spirit in which a composition is written must permeate it and be perceptible to any sensitive reader. The "Epipsychidion" has never been truly popular; should it ever become so, it would be a dire day, I think, to the English race. On the other hand, the day when "The Tempest" and "Comus" ceased to delight would be equally dire.

What has just been said of the advantages to be derived by creative writers from familiarity with the aims and methods of scientists applies with even greater force to critics and students of literature. Observation, combined with experiment, is the foundation stone of all the studies known as humane. As in the natural sciences, coördination of the results of study and speculation upon them are essential to progress; but that we may have results to work upon, observation of phenomena must precede. "Observe the facts in your chosen sphere of investigation" should be the first piece of advice given to the student of literature as well as to the student of chemistry, it being remembered, however, that a piece of literature, as a product of the human spirit, partakes of the

elusiveness of that spirit and hence cannot be
subjected to such complete analysis as is possible
in the case of a chemical product. But unless the
comparatively tangible characteristics of a literary
product are accurately observed and noted down,
there is no study of it in any true sense of the
term, for it is only on such observation, combined
with coördination and speculation, that any report
capable of carrying conviction to others can be
made on the product. This is a hard saying to
many persons who fancy that expatiating upon
the beauty of a poem is studying that poem.   It
is not.   It partakes much more of worship than
of investigation or study.   It may be better than
study, but it is not study, and its results may be
communicated, — enthusiasm is generally contagious, — but they cannot be taught, that is, made
objects of knowledge and of reasoned belief.

If this be so, it follows that the opposition
between scientific and literary studies in our institutions of learning should tend to disappear as
the true relations between science and literature
are better apprehended.   The student of literature is in his way a scientific observer, and his
prime object as student is the pursuit of truth.
As a lover of the beautiful and the good, — and,

as we have seen, he must be lover and student at the same time, — he uses literature in a different way, — he enjoys it, he derives noble ideals from it, he becomes through contact with it a better man. But he can succeed in being a true student and a true lover at one and the same time only on the terms by which it is possible for the scientist to be a true student and a true lover of the province of the universe with which he deals. Both must draw the proper distinction between what they know and what they feel. The temptation of the literary student to confound these is the greater, but he must manfully resist it. It is because so many critics and historians and students of literature fail to do this, that so much confusion and contradiction prevails in literary studies — to the amusement or the disgust of the scientist. It is quite possible, however, to study the facts of literature scientifically while enjoying æsthetically its beauties, and not to confound the two processes. Just so, the botanist can admire and enjoy the beauty of the flower he dissects. But neither the student of literature nor the student of botany will derive the full disciplinary value from his studies unless he bases them firmly upon systematic observation. This means that literary studies rest ultimately on the same basis as that sublime science, astronomy. We hitch our wagons to books instead of to stars; but, after all, books are the products of man's creative soul, and the soul of a man like Milton, as Wordsworth long since told us, is like a star. In the final analysis a drop of water is as wonderful as a star, and a book is as wonderful as either; and although our instruments of observation, when we play our parts as students of literature, are not so accurate as the microscope and the telescope, neither our fallible instruments nor the objects of our study will be underrated by the catholic mind.

But we come around so often to that one word "catholic" and the idea which underlies it, that it seems both needless and impertinent to continue this line of argument any further. He who once grasps the idea of catholicity does not need arguments to convince him of the futility of wrangling, of the narrow-mindedness implicit in the assumption that there can be real opposition between two great groups of mental pursuits. I will reason, therefore, no longer, and will conclude with an appeal to all who hear me to set their faces against every endeavor to advance any science at the expense of any art, or any art at the expense of

any science. Why cannot you, my biological
friend, gather your students around you in your
laboratory, and you, my colleague in Greek literature, read with your class the adventures of
Ulysses among the blameless Phæacians, without
having the unanswerable question raised, Which
of you is doing the more to advance the interests
of the race? That is a silly question to ask. A
proper question would be, When will sentimen-
talists cease to hamper the biologist in his experiments, and when will the state or generous
individuals give him every facility he needs in
the prosecution of his noble services to humanity?
Another proper question would be, When will
Philistines cease to make mere utilitarianism the
sole standard of life? in other words, When will
they cease to be Philistines, and therefore to be
obnoxious? To these questions, probably but one
answer can be given — Never! But they are not
profitless questions, because involved in each there
is an ideal to be striven for. Intellectual freedom
and generosity and sympathy are attainable by all,
and are beneficial to the entire race; but any
ungenerous rivalry between studies is founded in
selfishness, and is therefore base and to be eschewed. The picture of Nausicaa receiving the

shipwrecked Ulysses is as priceless a possession
of the human race as any discovery of science or
any achievement of statesman or soldier.[1] It is
an integral part of civilization, for if there had
been no Greek race capable of producing in its
dawn that Father of Poets upon whose inner eye
that ineffably lovely picture stamped itself, there
is no reason to believe that modern science would
be what it is, or that the annals of Western Europe
would have been rendered so illustrious by soldiers
and by statesmen. And if, furthermore, the day
should ever come when the world would consent
to drop from the category of desirable acquisitions
the knowledge of that Greek tongue in which
centuries ago that exquisite picture was unfolded
before the minds of barbarian chieftains by wandering bards, the heirs of Homer's art, then the
scientist would do well to break his instruments
and the statesman to close his books and his
portfolio; for the reign of chaos described by the
poet would have begun, and there would be nothing left for any lover of his kind but to exclaim,

> " Thy hand, great Anarch! lets the curtain fall,
> And universal darkness buries all."

[1] See the closing pages of this volume. The Sixth Book of the
"Odyssey" is a poetic creation, the beauty of which might well
turn a critic into a harper on one string.

VI
TEACHING LITERATURE

[Delivered as one of a series of public lectures during the Summer Session of Columbia University, July, 1902. Published in *The Sewanee Review* for October, 1904.]

VI

TEACHING LITERATURE

IT need scarcely be said that a fairly large literature, in a special sense of the term, has of late grown up around the question how literature in general should be taught. Whole books have been devoted to it, and the number of articles concerning it is rather formidable. I myself have written three such papers; but it is a subject that admits of much discussion, and I suppose that I am not exceptional in finding myself dissatisfied, in the light of accumulating experience, with much of my past theorizing and writing. For this reason, if for no other, I should like to examine the matter afresh.

To do this, we must reason from the bottom up; and we shall require working definitions of our two terms, "literature" and "teaching." No one has yet succeeded in defining "literature," but it is generally understood that, when used in connection with schools and colleges, to a less extent

with universities and the reading public, the scope of
the term "literature" is narrowed by the exclusion
of books that have little or no æsthetic value.   In
other words, only the books which through their
subject-matter or their style or through both please
us to a certain extent — that is, affect our emotions in a more or less agreeable way — are
counted as constituting "literature" in our sense
of the term.   These agreeable books are mainly
differentiated through the fact that they are full
of that indefinable something which we call "imagination " — that is to say, they fall chiefly under
the categories of poetry, drama, and fiction.   It is
furthermore evident, not merely that masses of
books, useful for various purposes, yet not capable
of giving much or any æsthetic pleasure, are excluded from literature, but that perhaps as many
more are shut out because, comparatively speaking,
they have ceased to please and are no longer literature for us.   This is equivalent to saying that time
does part of our winnowing for us.   The teaching
of literature means really the teaching, not of once
popular, but of classic books, and, in a few cases,
of such contemporary books as seem to possess
qualities likely to make them classic.

But what does the term "teaching" mean

when applied to a subject that involves our emotional natures ? Here is really the crucial point of our problem. Do we understand that, for us, to teach shall mean to inculcate, or that it shall mean to impart pleasure, or that it shall mean to instruct, or that it shall mean all three ? If we emphasize the idea of inculcation, we must obviously intend to give ourselves up chiefly to what I have elsewhere termed *teaching the spirit of literature* — to inculcating the higher and the lower virtues of humanity that in various ways are illustrated in the classical writings of our own literature and of foreign literatures. For example, we shall use Lowell's odes in order to inculcate the virtue of patriotism.

If we emphasize the idea of imparting delight, we must intend to give ourselves up to the task of training the æsthetic faculties of our pupils so that they may more fully appreciate the beauties of literature and learn more and more to take pleasure in the choicest books. For example, we shall use Lowell's odes in order to impart and develop the delight the trained ear receives from choice diction and harmonious rhythm. For many of us, to be sure, it is impossible to avoid combining inculcation of the humane virtues with this imparting of æsthetic delight; but it is possible greatly to emphasize the latter function of the teacher, since the giving of æsthetic pleasure is held by not a few critics to be the chief if not the sole reason for the existence of literature.

If, on the other hand, we emphasize the idea of instruction, we must obviously intend to give ourselves up, in the main, to teaching the facts of literature — that is, to dwelling upon literary history and biography, to laying stress on names and dates and periods, to tracing literary influences, to studying the evolution of a special form of composition; for example, the drama.   In brief, if we use literature as matter for inculcation, we teachers of it must take our stand, at least in part, with the preachers, the moralists; and if as a means of imparting delight, with the apostles of æsthetic culture; if, on the contrary, we use literature as matter for instruction, we must take our place with our friends who endeavor to convey a knowledge of the facts of language, of history, of economics, of the natural sciences.

But I doubt whether there are many teachers of literature who do not try to combine the methods involved in the phrases, to impart delight, to inculcate, and to instruct.   They use Lowell's odes to inculcate the virtue of patriotism, and to impart and develop æsthetic pleasure; but they also give instruction with regard to those facts of Lowell's life and of American history which explain how and why he came to write his odes, and to fill them with the patriotic spirit. Yet this does not get us so far away from our crucial point as we may imagine. The question of the proportions of inculcation and æsthetic training to be blended with one another and with instruction still remains to perplex us; and we are still confronted with the more difficult and certainly the more practical question of how we shall test the value of the instruction we convey. If we are to have our courses recognized as integral parts of the school or college curriculum, we must either hold our examinations and make our reports, as our friends — I will not call them rivals — do, or we must adopt other methods of advancing our students and must satisfy our fellow-teachers that we are not merely giving what are technically known in college slang as "snap courses."

I suppose my own experience in this matter has been that of many others. I have detected among my friends engaged in other forms of instruction a tendency to question the strict-

ness, the mental discipline, the definite, tangible
qualities of the work done in school and college
classes devoted to the study of literature.   Certainly this is the case with respect to English and
other modern literatures; the literatures of Greece
and Rome, having so long been used as material
for philological studies, have been less questioned
on the score of the strictness of the mental discipline derived from instruction in them, but have
not escaped censure on the score of general utility.
I do not believe that the doubts of these critical
teachers are unnatural, or that they will be
removed unless we succeed in doing one of two
things.   We must either impart such rigidity to
our tests of the amount and quality of our instruction as shall make it obvious that our
classes are as difficult to pass as those of any
teacher of another branch of study; or, by a
clear analysis of the theory of the teaching and
study of literature, we must convince all other
educators, and perhaps the public as well, that,
while literature is as important a study as any
other and must be included in any good school,
college, or university curriculum, the methods of
teaching it are of necessity fundamentally different from those employed in other studies and

warrant a wide departure from the normal tests of instruction.

Has any one made such an analysis of the theory of the teaching of literature as clearly sets that study apart from all others? If any one has, I have not seen it. On the other hand, has any one succeeded in imparting such rigidity to the methods of teaching literature and of testing the instruction conveyed as to make it plain that literature is as difficult and important a study as any other? I have no doubt that many persons have done this, at least so far as concerns the matter of difficulty. I have done it myself, and I can engage to "pitch" anybody else, or to get "pitched" myself, in an indefinite series of examinations. But, while we are imparting rigidity to our instruction, are we not in constant danger of forgetting our work of inculcation and of æsthetic training? Are we not further haunted by the thought that an extremely large proportion of the facts about literature that we make our pupils learn must be speedily forgotten by them, and can in few cases do them any direct good?

I confess I have been haunted by this thought for fifteen years. Ever since I had certain answers given me, which I am fond of repeating,

I have doubted the great value of instruction, not merely in the facts of literary history and biography, but in minute verbal exegesis. Ever since a student, remembering that *cynosure* is derived from the Greek for dog's tail, commented on the lines of "L'Allegro,"

> "Where perhaps some beauty lies,
> The cynosure of neighboring eyes,"

to the effect that they had something to do with a dog, I have been sceptical of the utility of much of the teaching that we feel obliged to examine upon. I have also been sceptical of many of the other tests of memory to which unfortunate children have been and are subjected — for example, of the tests of memory required of them in geography and grammar; but in geography and grammar the use of maps and examples helps the memory, whereas in literature there is little support given to the memory save by a comparatively few specimens of poetry and prose read in class and in private. Surely our brethren who teach the sciences have in their laboratories, in their experiments, a great advantage over us who can seldom bring our students into sufficient contact with the body of that literature about the history and minute details of which we propose to examine them more or less strictly.

But some one may say, " You are behind the times. Literature used to be taught from manuals and other dry-as-dust compilations; now we use carefully selected and edited texts, we have school libraries, we make our pupils do a considerable amount of outside reading. We require them to study up special topics and write essays upon them — in other words, we use 'laboratory methods.' "

So be it; yet I fancy that I have had a fair opportunity of watching the development of English instruction in this country. I can go back to the day when a little English grammar and a weekly composition or the recitation of a poem constituted the English work of many a well-regulated school. I can recollect when specific English chairs were first established in large universities. I well remember the leading features of English instruction during the decade from 1880 to 1890. It was almost entirely linguistic. Young doctors from German universities were returning in large numbers, the Johns Hopkins University was initiating German methods, and as a result it was difficult anywhere in the United States to secure specifically literary instruction. The text-books used in school and college alike were filled with notes tracing the history of words, and were singularly lacking, not merely in anything that would stimulate a pupil's love of literature, but often in anything that would give him an adequate idea of the place in literary history held by the author and book he was studying.

Late in the eighties and early in the nineties came the inevitable reaction — a small crusade against the neglect of literature in the universities and schools. The result was soon apparent. Philologians began to desire to prove themselves to be experts in literature as well, and issued some queer text-books. Specific chairs of literature were established, and soon some colleges and universities gave perhaps disproportionate attention to the new subject. The change was even more marked in the schools. Classes in English literature were added to the programme of studies, and a series of English classics was selected on which examinations for entrance into college were based. Latter-day school-teachers know the woes and the blessings attendant upon teaching those English classics better than I do, since, when I taught in schools, English literature was scarcely recognized as a fit subject of instruction — at least in the South.

But has this movement of the past ten years been as much of an advance as some of us who tried to help it on fondly imagined it would be? Are teachers of literature in possession of methods of teaching comparable in applicability and precision with those of other teachers? Are the pupils they teach satisfactorily trained? Is literature as a subject of instruction really on a par with other subjects of instruction?

To these questions varying answers will be given. I myself do not doubt that we have progressed, although I do doubt whether we have made much advance. I suspect that our methods are still very faulty, not merely because literature is a difficult subject to teach, but because we have not thoroughly analyzed our purposes or our means. I scarcely believe that literature, in spite of the increased attention given to it, is on a par with other subjects of instruction. And I even venture to question whether many boys and girls go to college with a greater knowledge and love of literature than was the case before they were drilled and examined in the redoubtable " English Classics." Observe that I do not question that our public schools have done something very useful in bringing into some contact with literature masses of children who a generation ago would have been left without that refining influence upon their lives. What I doubt is whether the generation now entering college, after a course of literature in the schools, is much better off, so far as a love and a knowledge of literature are concerned, than my own generation was with practically no training in the subject. The present generation, if it has been properly trained, ought to be a good deal better off; but while it is certainly a most athletic generation, to the muscular strength and dexterity of which I willingly pay tribute, it has not succeeded in making me feel that it knows much more about Shakspere and Milton and Byron and Shelley than we benighted youngsters did over twenty years ago.

What I am mainly concerned with, however, is the question from which I have wandered away — the question whether we teachers of literature can safely make our methods as rigid as those of other teachers, and, if we cannot, whether we can convince our brother teachers of the sciences and the semi-sciences that our methods must be radically different from theirs. This question with regard to rigidity of methods is an old one. The late Professor Freeman, the historian, violently opposed the establishment of a chair of literature at Oxford. "We cannot examine," he said, "in tastes and sympathies." To which Mr. Churton Collins replied: "No, examine in the *Poetics*, in the *Rhetoric*, in Quintilian's *Institutes*, in the *De Sublimitate*, in the *Laocoon*, and examine with the object of testing the results of such discipline." This was an excellent answer so far as postgraduate classes in criticism were concerned; but, as I pointed out over ten years ago in *The Sewanee Review*, Mr. Collins did very little to help school and college teachers of literature. These have to examine, let us say, in "The Merchant of Venice," not in Aristotle, Longinus, and Lessing. They do examine in the former, and, with the aid of the notes learned editors furnish, the examinations set may be made rigid enough to satisfy the most censorious critic. But at once we are thrown on the other horn of our dilemma. Do we not sacrifice the spirit of literature while we are examining on the letter, or rather training our poor children so that they may stand some other person's examination on the letter? As the dread day comes around, do teachers find themselves and their classes reading with rapt interest the noble speeches of Portia, or are they busy with the date of the play, with some critic's opinion with regard to Portia's womanliness, with the names and dates of act-ual women lawyers and law teachers in Italy, with the sources of the caskets incident, and similar matters only too dear to examiners?

I do not know how others feel about the matter, but I know that after about two years' firm grasp-ing of the rigid horn of the dilemma, if I may so express it, I began gradually to swing my-self over to the other horn — to what I may call the flexible horn. I began to doubt the value of strenuous examinations and to appre-ciate more and more the necessity of trying to inculcate in my students some of the high moral and spiritual truths taught by great writers, and to impart to them a taste for reading, a love of the best literature. In order to achieve this re-sult, even to a slight extent (and a slight success is all that I think any teacher should dare to hope for), I found that I must do much less in-structing — much less questioning with regard to the facts of literary history — and that I must do far more reading of authors than talking about them. I found also that it seemed advisable, in a college at least, to make a distinction between the younger and the older students — to treat the younger ones somewhat as I should treat high-school pupils, the older ones somewhat as I should treat postgraduate students. With the latter I adopted methods which need not be discussed here; with the former, methods which, if sound, should, it seems to me, be shared in the main by all teachers of literature in schools; for if our American college is anything, it is a halfway house, or station, between the high school and the university. In consequence, it should begin by continuing in considerable measure the methods of teaching used in the schools, and it should gradually change these methods so as to make them lead up to those of the university.

But my new treatment of my younger students led to some important results. Reading so much to them myself and giving them so much outside reading to do left no time for the study of a formal manual of literary history. As a text-book of that sort does little good if used by the pupil alone, it followed that I had to reduce to a minimum the study of the history of literature. I finally required the reading of Stopford Brooke's

excellent " Primer of English Literature," but did
not examine on it. I knew well enough that I was
making a sacrifice on the side of exact knowledge,
but it seemed to me it had to be made. There
were other sacrifices requisite. I like to criticise,
I like to theorize, and I have my favorite authors,
some of whom are not specially suited to the comprehension and needs of young people. I found
that only the most general and obvious kind of
criticism was possible under my new system, that
much theorizing was out of the question, and that
often the books I should never have thought
of taking down from my shelves for my own
delectation were precisely the ones I ought to
take down for the delectation and profit of my
students. This is merely to say that I learned by
bitter experience that the teacher must sacrifice
to his students his preferences, his prejudices, his
time, almost everything except his enthusiasm and
such other traits as make him a real individual.
A mere repeater of other people's thoughts, a man
or woman who has no standards, no decided points
of view, will certainly fail as a teacher; but so I
think will the man or woman who is not willing to
sacrifice prejudices and preferences, and to sympathize with the tastes and needs of students.

Let me illustrate my meaning by a concrete incident. I had an excellent assistant once, to whom,
however, I had to give one mild scolding. I happened to overhear him making fun of Scott's
poetry to a class of boys, few of whom were
over seventeen. Neither that assistant nor myself was at the age when " The Lady of the
Lake" is a surpassing delight; but those boys
were, and I expostulated with the jocular teacher.
He could scarcely have displayed greater fatuity,
unless he had imitated a bit of fatuity I myself
had been guilty of a few years before — that is,
ridiculing Longfellow. It is scarcely necessary to
say that teaching should almost invariably be positive rather than negative in character. It should
bring out the merits of the book studied rather
than its defects. It should aim to develop in
children a catholic taste for everything that is
good in literature, rather than to encourage prejudices, although a prejudice in favor of an author
or a book should be dealt with cautiously. This is
but to say that the good teacher of literature must
have many of the qualifications requisite to a good
critic — he must be sympathetic, healthy in his
tastes, sound in his judgments, and fairly well
read.

But the teacher who devotes himself mainly to wide and sympathetic reading with his classes, who rarely instructs but continually endeavors by direct and indirect means to inculcate humane virtues and develop æsthetic tastes — in other words, to instil into his pupils a love of the books that illustrate those virtues and exercise those tastes — must be prepared to make other sacrifices. He must be prepared, as I have said, to sink his own preferences for special books and to use such as will best suit his pupils. He must also be willing to rely on his own judgment rather than on the judgments of others, even of omniscient college professors. If the annotated texts furnished him do not produce the best results, he must eschew their use as far as he may. Personally I have found such texts occasionally valuable, but I prefer Palgrave's " Golden Treasury of Songs and Lyrics "[1] to any annotated text I ever used, and that delightful anthology, I need scarcely say, is one that every teacher should be glad to take down from his shelves for his own enjoyment.

[1] It is a pleasure to notice that the larger part of this book has been added to the list of volumes that may be read by pupils preparing for college, and that teachers now have a wider range of books to select from. But it is the methods rather than the materials of instruction that are chiefly in question.

But the teacher must often make a sacrifice of part of what may be called his technical equipment. Most of us are trained to question our students systematically and to make use of the tests furnished by oral and written examinations. Yet I do not see, any more than Professor Freeman did, how the teacher can examine on tastes and sympathies, how he can ask questions about the humane virtues, without running great risk of making his students prigs, and himself — what shall I say? — a canting Pharisee? Perhaps that is too strong — let me say a plain fool. I believe it to be very foolish to make young people self-conscious with regard to spiritual and æsthetic things by insisting upon their talking and writing about them. It is still more foolish to think that one can satisfactorily mark and grade their answers on such topics.

But some one may ask: "Can we not examine on the facts we instruct in, and require essays on the spiritual and æsthetic matters we inculcate and impart? By means of a combination of marks for diligence and interest shown in class work, for success in written examinations, and for ability displayed in the composition of themes and essays, can we not grade our pupils in a thoroughly satisfactory manner?"

So far as marks for diligence and interest in class work are concerned, I fancy that no school superintendent or principal or fellow-teacher in another study will deny that a good teacher of literature is able to grade his pupils satisfactorily. So far as advancement in school or college is dependent upon such grading, which is itself dependent upon the judgment of the individual teacher, I cannot see that literature stands on a markedly different footing from other studies. With regard to examinations on the facts of literary history and biography, I suppose their disciplinary value is not less than that of examinations in many other studies. Their value as a means to store the mind with useful and available knowledge is more questionable, and, although literature means much to me personally, I am obliged to confess that I doubt whether it is not outranked by most other studies as a body of useful and available knowledge. As matters stand, teachers must examine in it. The colleges require entrance examinations and will continue for some time to require them — whether or not a few unfashionable people like myself think they have made too much of a fetich of their written tests.

I gladly admit that probably the required examinations on English texts have done good in making room for the study of English literature in schools, and that as a temporary expedient the establishment of the system was warranted. But I think that a radical change in the methods of preparing boys and girls for college is called for, — so far at least as English is concerned, — since I doubt whether more or less rigid examinations in literature now help the colleges or the school-teachers greatly, and I suspect they help the unfortunate pupils still less. I doubt if any of us knows so clearly as the teacher of mathematics does, for example, in his specialty, what amount of knowledge of literary history and biography, and of metrical, linguistic, and rhetorical facts needed in literary studies, a Freshman should possess on entering college. I doubt whether any of us can be truly said to be very sapient with regard to the best methods of conveying this unknown minimum of instruction, — for that there should be *some* instruction in these matters is clear, — and I also doubt

whether most of the instruction we do attempt
does not frequently act as a deterrent from the
true comprehension and enjoyment of literature.
I will even go so far as to say that at present I
should prefer to admit to college on positive
tests in composition, rhetoric, and grammar, —
in other words, on tests relating to the use of
the vernacular, — and on the statement by the
teacher that the pupil had done a wide amount
of reading under direction.

For it is wide reading that best develops any
native love of literature, that is most likely to
bring out a latent love for it, and that not infrequently leads to the attainment of a greater
knowledge of the facts of literary history and
biography than is often secured through cut-and-
dried methods of instruction.   It is a lack of
fairly wide reading on the part of students and
a certain inflexibility of taste resulting from
narrow reading and faulty literary instruction
that hamper me more than anything else in
teaching college classes.   It is this same lack
of wide reading that chiefly discourages postgraduate students during the first year of their
university course and that renders so many of
their dissertations jejune and amateurish.   I grant

that the school and college curriculums are so
crowded that it is almost unfair to expect of
pupils and students as much general reading
as was done by some of my contemporaries;
but I believe that if the annotation employed
in the school classics were reduced in amount,
and if examinations in literature in school or
college were either done away with or minimized, the time saved might be profitably employed in reading. The amount and quality of
this reading could be at least fairly tested — not
so well, perhaps, by concrete questions, which
might be anticipated by the pupil, as by the
intelligence with which certain passages were
read aloud. This would not be a conclusive
test. The bright pupil willing to be dishonest
could easily pretend to have read more than
he had done; but is any test that can be de-
vised sufficiently flexible to catch bright dishonest
pupils without being unfair to less bright and
more honest ones?

Whether now the school authorities would be
satisfied to admit to the programme of studies a
subject in which no examinations were held,
even if the colleges waived entrance examinations on it, is a point on which I have no

data for forming an opinion. I should think, however, that a fairly satisfactory system of grading could be built up on marks for diligence, which are in the nature of conduct marks, and on the time spent on reading in class as well as on the hours presumably covered by the outside reading. Such a system of grading could also take into account the character of the reading aloud done by the pupil; and on the intelligence displayed in this, on the general diligence vouched for by the teacher, and on the time devoted to reading by the pupil I should imagine that all questions relating to advancement could be determined satisfactorily to parents, principals, and fellow-teachers. Such satisfaction would naturally depend upon all parties concerned being made to see clearly that rigid examinations and other tests in literary studies not only do little positive good, but are really harmful as lessening the teacher's opportunities to inculcate and train rather than to instruct, and as boring pupils and putting a barrier between them and that body of literature with which it is most essential that they should be brought into frequent and prolonged contact. If, finally, written tests must be set in order not to disturb too violently the school machinery, why should it not be understood that all examinations in literature would be graded on the interest, diligence, and general intelligence shown by the pupil, and on his ability to write correct English, rather than on his knowledge of facts about literature, except as regards that unknown minimum of instruction about which a word will be said later? Such examinations would supplement those given in English composition, would throw fresh light upon the character and mental attainments of each pupil, and would assist in the determination of all questions relative to advancement. They would also furnish those ocular evidences of a pupil's immaturity or unwillingness to apply himself that are so needed by teachers whenever their decisions are disputed.

But the third sort of test mentioned above remains to be considered — the test furnished by the writing of frequent essays. This is much favored by some teachers, and it is doubtless successful when the pupil has an aptitude for writing. But that aptitude is comparatively rare, and I am not sure that essay-writing is not nearly or quite as bad for most young people as rigid examinations in literature are likely to be. In this particular I fear I am a grievous heretic. Neatly written essays are such gentlemanly and ladylike things — especially when they are tied with ribbons. I always feel as if I were highly honored when a nice young man or woman presents me with the product of many hours' study and creative energy, particularly when it is typewritten and of moderate length. When the writer is a person of some maturity, a graduate student who has done either a small or a large amount of individual research, I examine the essay with pleasure, both because I very frequently learn something I am glad to know and because I feel that I may be of service in directing a bent for study which I presume to exist from the fact that the graduate student has taken the trouble to enter as a candidate for a higher degree.

But for the school or college essay used as a test of literary work rather than as a test of work in English composition, I must confess I have very little respect. I fear that it encourages smattering, that it stimulates juvenile conceit, that it tends to crystallize tastes and opinions at an age when every effort should be made to widen and lend flexibility to the mind, that it leads to unconscious plagiarism and to a complacent habit of airing one's commonplaceness and fatuity.

I wish to avoid seeming extreme, but I must say
that American schools and colleges have in my
judgment set far too high a premium upon essay-
writing. I gather from some remarks of Mr.
Frederic Harrison that this has been done in
England also, and I am glad that in Mr. Harrison
I find at least one sharer of my pessimistic views
with regard to the future of a race that is encouraged from its earliest youth to write itself down
with Dogberry. I have no quarrel, of course,
with the theme or essay employed as a means to
improve a student's use of his mother tongue; I
have no quarrel with it employed as a means to
develop the critical powers and the literary tastes
of students who in one way or another have given
evidence of aptitude for the study of letters; I
have no quarrel with the essay or written report
used moderately in connection with classes in
literature, especially in universities. What moves
me to wrath is our national habit of requiring
graduation theses of Harry and Lucy, no matter
whether they want to write them or not, and of
insisting that they inflict them upon adult audi-
ences. I am also moved to pity, when I see teachers loaded down with bundles of essays on literary
topics which they have conceived it to be their

duty to demand from every member of their classes. I cannot help believing that nine out of ten of those essays give no real evidence of any higher power than that of extracting jejune information from encyclopædias and from the writings of other people. The tenth, perhaps, gives evidence of something better; but cannot the teacher find out this tenth student without making the other nine dish up a hebdomadal hash of platitudes?

Any teacher who will not encourage and guide any student honestly desirous of learning how to write upon literary topics is unworthy of the name of teacher. Any man of letters who does not remember that he was once a neophyte himself, and gladly give what help he can to a competent young man or woman purposing to enter upon a literary life, is unworthy of the standing he has obtained. But the teacher or man of letters who encourages every one, regardless of natural aptitude, to write literary essays upon every possible occasion seems to me to be doing little good either to the individual encouraged or to the cause of education. If the amount of time spent by average school children and college students in consulting encyclopædias and compiling essays were devoted to good reading, I fancy that the cause of culture would be greatly subserved. I would give every child the chance to develop whatever faculty it may have for writing — just as I would give it the chance to develop its presumptive faculty for drawing, for music, and for the other arts — but I think that this should be done by the teacher of composition, who can easily call in the teacher of literature to lend his aid should the case seem to require it. For the teacher of literature, however, to divert his energies from his greatest task of inculcating a love of wide reading to inculcating in Harry and Lucy a desire to see themselves in print or to hear themselves on a commencement platform is to me at least a most questionable procedure.[1] And surely the mere knowledge amassed by the essay writer does not compensate for the injury that may be done him in the ways I have mentioned.

I cannot forbear suggesting here, at the risk of being accused of impertinence in discussing matters about which I am not expert, that latter-

[1] Some relief seems to be in sight, especially in the large universities, probably in part on account of the size of their graduating classes. Columbia has for some years heard no student orations on commencement day and has just (1905) ceased to require graduation theses.

day teachers of composition have as many fundamental problems to solve as confront teachers of literature. It is very doubtful, as some of the inaugurators of the modern "theme-courses" confess, whether the expensive and time-consuming methods of teaching boys and girls to write with something approaching a style have produced results at all commensurate with the labor expended. Perhaps it has not been realized that all instruction in composition after the pupil has been trained, if he can be, to write a short series of coherent and intelligible paragraphs, fairly idiomatic and free from blunders, — a not discreditable letter, for example, — is at bottom, so far as concerns style, instruction in an art. It follows that the experience and practice of the world in the matter of teaching the fine arts should be carefully studied by the teacher of the higher grades of composition. We are beginning to see, as I have just intimated, that it is only fair to any child to give it an opportunity to show whether it has any aptitude for music, drawing, and the other arts. Just so, I repeat, we ought to give and are giving our children an opportunity in the elementary courses in composition to show whether they have in them the faintest desire or capacity to do creative writing and to acquire the rudiments of a style. It would be sheer folly, however, to keep a boy or girl at the study of music or drawing to the age of twenty or thereabouts when not a trace of aptitude for either art had ever been apparent in them. Is it particularly wise to encourage equally incompetent students of the art of writing to manufacture short stories or sets of verses or essays or book reviews — especially to do this at the expense of training in old-fashioned, but not useless, formal rhetoric? Cannot some of the "required" hours in English during the Freshman and Sophomore years be saved for reading under the supervision of an instructor skilled in pointing out stylistic features, and ought we not to recognize the fact that, save in exceptional cases, the proper affiliations of good work in advanced composition are with logic rather than with the fine arts. For one good story-teller or essayist turned out by our colleges they might furnish us, I suspect, a hundred good debaters, if they only would.

Perhaps I ought to give two experiences I have had in this connection that will help to explain the strong language I have employed. I shall not soon forget the disgust I felt when an old teacher of mine — a most admirable man in many ways — once told his class complacently how he had won a prize of fifty dollars for an essay on Chaucer. He had never read a line of that great poet, but he took "Poole's Index," read up his subject in various magazine articles, and was clever enough to win the prize. He told us that story with pride, and practically said to each one of us, "Go thou and do likewise." It seemed to me that although he had not cut off his hand before writing that essay, he ought to have cut out his tongue before boasting about it. Yet how much smattering and intellectual dishonesty similar to his must have been fostered in this country by the givers of prizes, the assigners of essays, the conductors of literary clubs!

My second experience was more amusing and less nauseating. I used, years ago, to be pestered by a worthy but very immature student to give him bibliographies that would help him to write essays on Dante, Petrarch, and other great poets of whose works I knew he had never read a line. The same student was acting as private secretary to one of my friends, and, whenever his employer went out, this youthful essayist would go to the front door and hail passers-by with the request that they would spell for him words of two or more syllables that occurred in the letters he had to typewrite. I am not, I believe, niggardly of my time where students are concerned; but the incursions of that young man into my study for books on Italian literature, when he should have asked to borrow a Webster's Spelling Book, tried my patience sorely.

Now a word in conclusion with regard to that unknown minimum of knowledge of literary history and biography, and of metrical, rhetorical, and linguistic facts, which a Freshman should be presumed to possess on entering college. My language here must be very tentative, for I must confess that the topic is one that has long puzzled me sorely. As for the metrical, rhetorical, and linguistic facts, it would be a comfort to rely for instruction in them on the teacher of English composition. As for the literary history and biography, it would be a comfort to rely on the teacher of history proper; for literature is a part of culture, and we must sooner or later wake up to the fact that culture-history should share with political and military history the attention of school children. But I doubt whether the teachers of history and of composition will care to have their

labors greatly increased, and I suppose we must
blunder along until some one writes us a common
sense " Introduction to the Study of Literature "
in which this minimum of positive knowledge is
conveyed in an agreeable fashion.

But I have promulgated heresies enough for one
paper. I have frankly stated my belief that the
time devoted to spiritual inculcation and to æsthetic
training is of far more importance than that devoted to instruction in the facts of literature, and
I draw hence the conclusion that we teachers of
literature ought bravely to say to our fellow-
teachers something like this : " We can, if we
please, make our examinations as rigid as you do
yours, but we do not believe that our facts are as
important as yours, or at any rate that they may
be acquired with so much advantage to our pupils.
We wish to grade and advance our pupils on more
flexible lines than you adopt, because we believe
that the nature of our subject makes such flexible
lines advisable. We believe that both the subject
we teach and the subjects you teach are necessary
to a catholic education ; but that, while we are
contributing to the same end as you, our means
must be different from yours."

Some such appeal, accompanied by friendly

discussion, will, I am sure, in time satisfy every intelligent person that no harm to school discipline will be done if the teaching of literature finally resolves itself into little more than securing a wide amount of reading from children during their school years. It will, I trust, in time satisfy the colleges that the examinations they now hold on selected English classics are more or less useless and should be modified or dropped. Finally, I hope that the study we must all give to the problems connected with the teaching of literature will sooner or later lead us — I will not say to became teetotalers with regard to our national dissipation in essay-writing — but at least moderate in our use of that seductive form of mental titillation. When I see young ladies and gentlemen armed with their numerous and formidable essays, I am irresistibly reminded of the young woman who drank so many cups of tea that the elder Mr. Weller was compelled to exclaim that she was "a swellin' wisibly." I seem to see the young lady and gentleman essayists "swellin' wisibly" with mental pride. Let us have fewer new bad essays written and more good old books read.[1]

[1] I may be permitted, I trust, to express here my gratification at the notice taken of this article by *The Dial*, *The Evening Post*,

and other journals, and also to thank the persons who wrote me expressing their sympathy with my views. One letter in particular from Dean Sidney Edward Mezes of the University of Texas contained a passage which I extract, with the writer's permission.

" One suggestion in a matter of detail I wish to make, to meet the objection, on the part of teachers of other subjects, that literature without examinations or other tests is a 'snap.' Why might not the literature classes meet with the instructor for twice or even three times as many hours as other classes that count equally toward degrees? This would put them, in important respects, on a par with laboratory courses, and, I think, would do away with the objection mentioned."

Certainly, if the cost of such extra instruction could be met and if the additional hours were secured equitably to all parties and studies concerned, no believer in the good effects of adequate instruction in literature would be likely to demur to Dean Mezes's suggestion.

VII

SOME REMARKS ON MODERN
BOOK–BURNING

[Read in part before the English Club of Amherst College, April 27, 1905.]

VII

SOME REMARKS ON MODERN BOOK-BURNING

I

I HAVE just been reading for the first time James Anthony Froude's notorious rather than famous religious story, "The Nemesis of Faith, or, The History of Markham Sutherland." This far from ponderous or formidable deliverance of a brilliant young Oxford deacon, who had passed from under the sway of Newman only to experience soon that of Carlyle and, to a less extent, that of Emerson, went through two editions, and then, save for an American reprint of 1880, practically disappeared from public attention for fifty-four years. In 1903 the story was reissued with an introduction by Mr. Moncure D. Conway, and it was this resuscitation, together with an anecdote Mr. Conway tells, that prompted me to make it a text for the present discussion.

As a piece of fiction the book, though not commonplace, is thin enough. It consists of ten letters from a young man describing how he had lost his hold on Christianity, how he is persuaded to take orders, how he fails as a priest. Then follow some of this Markham Sutherland's reflections on religious topics, then his "Confessions of a Sceptic," and, in conclusion, a friendly hand describes his miserable fate. Seeking health and peace of mind in Italy, he encounters a married woman to whom he becomes devoted, and whose love he wins because she has never loved her husband — a gentleman who displays singular obtuseness in the whole affair. The lovers stop short of adultery; but the woman's little daughter falls into a mortal illness, partly through their negligence; they are racked by remorse; and each dies miserable — under the shadow of the Church of Rome.

Of immoral intent the book was plainly innocent; of noxious effect it must have been almost equally innocent. Historical and philosophical doubts with regard to the truth of the Christian mysteries were in the air, as the Transcendental Movement in America and, in the opposite sense, the reactionary Tractarian Movement

in England had plainly shown, and as Tennyson's
" In Memoriam" was conclusively to prove the next
year.   Froude set forth his hero's doubts with not
a little learning and with more eloquence — indeed, there are two brilliant pages descriptive of
the " Pagani, Pagans, the old country villagers"
loyal to their gods, which the later master of English prose might have owned with pride.   But
his book was amorphous, it shifted its centre of
interest, it was over-hospitable to purple passages
of rhetoric — in short, it was too full of youthful
faults to shake the faith of many souls in stolid
England.   The question of morals raised by its
closing pages — to wit, the innocence or guilt
of the love given by a married woman to the
first man who has truly touched her heart — was
undoubtedly offensive to many persons, especially in view of the fact that Froude was a deacon and a fellow at Oxford ; but his handling of
the delicate situation was surely not such as to
increase the number of separations and divorces.

What chiefly strikes one on reading this sup-
posedly advanced, if not incendiary, book of 1849,
is how far it falls short of what would be deemed
shockingly radical in 1905.   Since " The Nemesis
of Faith " was first published, Darwin and Spencer

and the philosophy of evolution have had to be reckoned with, to say nothing of the highest claims of the so-called "higher criticism"; yet Faith is still far from admitting that she has seen her Nemesis, whether in sober treatise or in persuasive story. Since Froude's book, "Robert Elsmere" and many another religious novel have come and gone; and the limits of the fiction of passion have been pushed back almost far enough to satisfy a Frenchman. Mr. James's cracked "Golden Bowl" may, for aught I know, be symbolical of the disastrous fate awaiting, if it has not overtaken, that singular product of art, the English novel for family consumption.

But, as if men could never learn the lesson that denunciation and persecution are the most effective forms of propaganda, as if they could never see that any manifestation of hatred is likely to produce results unforeseen and undesired in a world in which the law of love is almost as potent and universal in the moral sphere as that of gravitation is in the physical sphere, this youthful manifesto of scepticism met a fate at Oxford at the middle of the nineteenth century not so very different from what it would have encountered at Rome or at Geneva at the middle of the sixteenth. "Froude's novel," says Mr. Conway, "must be introduced to the twentieth century with the distinction of being the only book piously burnt at Oxford in the nineteenth century. On February 27, 1849, a few weeks after its publication, Professor Sewell, lecturer in Exeter College, vehemently denounced the work in his lecture, and, discovering that a student present had a copy before him, seized it furiously and dashed it into the hall fire. In 1892, when Froude was appointed Regius Professor of Modern History at Oxford, some efforts were made to relieve the university of all responsibility for this conduct of a professor whose subsequent career was not honorable. But the university made itself a passive accessory by uttering no protest. Froude was a fellow of the college in which the incident occurred, and immediately sent in his resignation. Exeter College saw its ablest fellow driven out without a word of protest. His friend Clough soon after resigned his fellowship in Balliol, no doubt feeling that Oxford was no place for him if Froude could be dishonored there with impunity."

The immediate result was, of course, the sale of the entire edition. A less immediate but almost equally inevitable result was that Professor William Sewell is to-day known, if at all save to theologians, chiefly through his absurd attention to the Exeter Hall fire of half a century ago, and that, in consequence, the fact that he could not pay his debts, and was forced to take up his residence on the Continent, like some of Thackeray's shady characters, is remembered whenever his name is recalled. Doubtless, as Mr. Conway says, he would not have acted so foolishly if he had not been outraged, not merely by Froude's heresies, but by the latter's failure to take an orthodox attitude toward the moral or immoral relations of his hero and heroine. The man who compounds for sins he is inclined to by damning those he has no mind to has been a sufficiently familiar phenomenon from Adam to Butler, from Butler to Sewell, and from Sewell to us. It is only fair to add that Professor Sewell's debts seem to have been incurred in founding a high church college and a similar school, so that Mr. Conway's unqualified assertion of his "notorious laxity in money affairs" does him an injury which, in a sense, is only poetic justice.

But all this does not prove that Professor Sewell, though a book-burner, was a biblio-

phobe.   Himself the author of at least four
novels, of reviews and sermons and theological
tracts and treatises, he must have been, not
merely a scholar, but something of a man of
letters.   I must frankly say that I have no intention of taking the time and pains to determine whether I am correct in my suspicion that,
if I may parody Pope, he was one of those people
who to books repair, not for the pleasure but the
doctrine there.   His action in the lecture room
that day leaves him exposed to the charge that,
at times at least, he was more anxious to have a
book give support to his own views than to have it
exhibit all the literary virtues.   But, at bottom,
the man who cares only for the books that ex-
pound and defend the causes he espouses is
really a foe, and a very dangerous one, to literature.

He is in much the position of the man who is
pleasant to his friends and works with his party
or his church, but is destitute of the truly humane
spirit because he is not broad-minded and large-
hearted enough to sympathize with the stranger
and the alien.   He that is not for us is against
us is a saying that has a far wider application
than we are generally aware of.   Not to be for

our race is to be really against it — it is to be essentially selfish and self-centred, even when "self" is stretched to include social set, and college, and church, and party, and town, and state, and nation. So it is with literature and art and all the things of the mind. Not to be for them all — however slightly in our poor finiteness we may comprehend their full scope and adequately share the pleasures every mental pursuit yields those that love it — is, surely, in the final analysis, to be not a little against them. It is, at least, to limit that sympathy which every true artist and student may claim as his right from the fellow-men in whose behalf he labors; and by as much as the world's stock of sympathy is lessened, by so much is the way of the altruistic lover of the true, the beautiful, and the good made more arduous. Milton's aphorism might truly run — "As well not love a good man as not love a good book."

But Professor Sewell doubtless thought very honestly that Froude's book was a thoroughly bad one. It is just here that his example should serve as a warning — of a sort perennial, indeed, but apparently always necessary. The book that seems bad to us is so likely to seem innocuous, if not positively good, to a later generation. We are so prone to be hard and fast in our demands upon books and writers that the risk of doing them serious injustice is very great. With a little experience we can learn fairly well, I think, to pick out the trivial, the insincere, the positively obscene, the coarsely irreverent. No reader, for example, of some of Rochester's poems has at any time for two centuries and a quarter been at a loss for a verdict as to their essential immorality. But when the offence against morals ceases to be so plain that it can be dealt with under positive statutes, and when the triviality and insincerity are not vouched for in plain ways, — for example, by the low type of periodical or publisher responsible for their affronting the sun, — the lessons of literary history teach us that we should be exceedingly careful in asserting that any book is foolish or vicious. But does not experience tell us that we ought to be just as careful with regard to thinking such things about any man whom we have had no opportunity thoroughly to study? We are careful not to say or write such things about men, for the libel suit remains where the horsewhipping has disappeared. But how often we think them and later discover the injustice we have done; and how often we think and say and

write things about books and authors that we live
to be ashamed of !

I know I am telling a twice-told tale, but it will
surely bear repetition, as long as scientific and
artistic and theological and political partisanship
may be everywhere seen among men. History
teaches us that the accursed of to-day may be —
perhaps, is likely to be — the blessed of to-morrow;
yet we continue to curse and excommunicate and
to fancy that in so doing we are sending up grateful incense to the God of peace and love. We
fancy that we thereby show our zeal for the true,
the beautiful, and the good, when we are only
giving a needless additional illustration of how
aptly the theory of the simian descent of man fits
the facts of human life. We seem somehow to
think that our manhood is proportional to the
positiveness of our opinions upon disputed points,
much as some people appear to regard war as
a heaven-appointed agent for making men and
nations brave. That partisans may be manly and
lovers of war brave no intelligent person will deny;
but it is safer to affirm that the catholic-minded
man is the more manly and the lover of peace the
braver.

There is no need to dwell further on the matter,

save to say that the Professor Sewells have by no
means disappeared, even from this so-called liberal
country of ours. Every now and then some clergyman makes himself conspicuous by denounc-
ing the godless character of modern learning;
some artist, equally ignorant of what men are
doing outside his own sphere of activity, declares
that a great university is destitute of idealism, or
that the public is far sunk in bourgeois insensibility
and imbecility. Worse still, books dealing with
politics and economics in a fashion that does not
accord with the notions prevailing in this or that lo-
cality are made the objects of popular clamor, while
their authors are fortunate if they do not lose social
position and, in some cases, the means of livelihood. The thoughtless public and newspapers of
the baser sort fan these, it must be confessed,
comparatively mild flames of persecution. This is
not surprising, and it will continue for many a day.
What is more surprising and more pitiful is to see
an entire college or university faculty stand quiet,
as Exeter College stood, when one of its members
is denounced for exercising his right to think and
to express in reputable language the results of his
thinking. Fortunately, it is not always thus. In
a New England state noted for its political corrup-

tion, one college faculty in quite recent times has stood out in a most manly fashion for freedom of speech in politics and economics — even for freedom to utter what many of its members regarded as the grossest of economic heresies.

It behooves most of us, however, to remember that, even when we do not cast books we deem obnoxious into the fire, even when we do not join in the outcry against their writers, we are still partakers of the sin, or the fault, or whatever we may call it, of the bibliophobe, of the man who does not love books and literature enough to trust them in their beneficent work of enlightening the world, who sets up his small prejudices against the dictates of charity and the lessons of history. " He that is not for me is against me; " he that is silent when freedom is threatened and assailed is in his heart a slave. The rights of books is but another phrase for the rights of man; the active bibliophobe, if he were not so silly and comparatively harmless, would be as loathsome as a tyrant; the passive bibliophobe, as despicable as a thrall. And let us remember that bibliophobia and tyranny join hands when, as in these United States within the past ten years, it is seriously proposed, in the press and in conversation, to punish as traitors men who

deem it their duty to denounce the foreign policy
of the majority toward alien races.

II

Professor Sewell seems to have lineal descend-
ants, or, at least, disciples, in America. Not long
ago the newspapers printed a despatch from one
of our Western towns which described how a certain clergyman thought it proper to burn in a
stove in the centre of his church, before his awe-
struck or snickering congregation, the writings of
certain authors whom the world has long looked
upon with favor. Among the writers thus consigned to the flames in the persons of their books
— long after their bones had been consigned to
earth and their souls, I fear, in the opinion of our
good clergyman, to fiercer flames than those of his
stove — were William Shakspere and George
Gordon, Lord Byron. Most of the persons who
read the despatch were, naturally, tempted to smile
at this recrudescence of the spirit which led the
English Puritans to smash cathedral windows —
indeed, the despatch would not have been sent out
to the newspapers of the country if the minister's
performance had not been deemed erratic enough

to furnish food for a small amount at least of national merriment. It is a form of amusement not infrequently vouchsafed us. For example, a rather distinguished and somewhat venerable American poet, in discussing the decline of popular interest in poetry, has lately enlarged upon what he considers the overweening and overshadowing influence of Shakspere and Milton, who, he thinks, have no real message for our day, with its special problems, and whom, accordingly, he berates severely. It is not, however, the element of amusement involved in these and similar acts and expressions of opinion on which I wish to comment for a moment; it is rather the serious element that can be discovered in them.

I doubt whether it is safe to set down, as some people are often inclined to do, ebullitions of puritanism such as that of the Western clergyman, to the only too common desire to make one's self conspicuous in one way or another. It is by no means certain that this latest book-burner fondly hoped that he would be remembered as a second Omar — granting that Omar really did destroy the Alexandrian Library — or as a second Erostratus, — the vain person, it will be remembered, who, on the night Alexander the Great was born, set fire to the famous temple of Diana at Ephesus merely that he might be remembered for his crime, — a purpose more signally accomplished in his case than many a better one has been. Perhaps our zealous Westerner never heard of Erostratus or of Omar or of Professor Sewell, though he doubtless knew that it used to be the custom to burn in public books deemed to be pernicious. He apparently forgot that it was the public hangman that usually performed this questionable service.

No, I do not think that his extraordinary action proceeded from vanity. I suspect that he was merely doing what we are all continually doing, or ought to be doing, — simply trying to square his own soul with its environment and by his example to help other souls to square themselves. Life to that man was largely a question of following literally certain straight lines of conduct laid down by his religion and of holding tenaciously certain tenets laid down by his church, and he not only found little or nothing in the works of Shakspere and Byron that helped him to do this, but he found many a page dealing with lust and crime in a way that repelled his simple soul and hindered him from following the lines of conduct and opinion which in his judgment lead to eternal life. Once pos-

sessed of such an idea, what should a good pastor
do but seek to warn his flock in the most impressive manner possible against the dangers he had
discovered and shunned? He should not have
been so narrow-minded, we reply; he should not
have been so conceited as to set up his individual
opinion of Shakspere against that of the educated world; he should have possessed some at
least of the elements of humor.

But given his environment, given his opportunities of culture, how could he have been anything
else than narrow-minded, and how many narrow-
minded bigots of one sort or another there are in
America and in the world, and how far do we ourselves escape being narrow-minded in one respect
or another? How many of us are absolutely
broad-minded in politics, in our social relations, in
our tastes and sympathies in matters of religion
and art and literature? Suppose the injunction
were given us, "Let him who is without small-
mindedness be the first to sneer or laugh at this
preacher taken in the act of burning Shakspere," how many of us would be inclined to
indulge in scorn or hilarity? It was precisely
because he was narrow-minded and earnest that
he set his own judgment over against that of the

world and made himself appear ridiculously conceited. It was precisely because he was the product of a cramped and cramping environment, that he did not have that saving sense of humor which often, though by no means always, prevents us from doing things as ridiculous in their way as burning the works of Byron in a church stove. To say that such a man should not have been narrow, conceited, and lacking in humor is to say that he should not have been himself, — that is, that he should not have been the product of several centuries of lower middle class Philistinism.

And not only was this primitive-minded pastor in all probability acting in good faith and in accordance with all the light he had, but he was answering in his own way a question the world has been putting to itself for ages, viz., What should be the attitude of the man who believes that conduct is three-fourths or more of life toward the arts that to a greater or less degree influence conduct, and what responsibilities rest upon the artist in this regard? A tremendously puzzling question it has proved to be — one that has never been fully answered, one that cannot, perhaps, be answered save in a halting and a partial manner. Plato, as we all know, excluded most of the poets from his " Republic " — for reasons, much less crudely expressed, but not certainly wiser, than those of his latest follower. Milton, though he had likened the killing of a good book to the killing of a good man, did not altogether escape a few years later, especially with regard to Shakspere himself, from showing some, at least, of the moral intolerance displayed by Plato in the third and tenth books of his " Republic." On the other hand, — particularly in our own day, — certain artists and critics have passed to the opposite extreme, and, preaching from the text, " Art for art's sake," have practically proclaimed that to consider the effects of art upon conduct is a piece of impertinence toward art and artists. Between these two extremes men have wandered up and down seeking a plain path to follow. Their common sense tells them that to read bad books is but another way of keeping bad company, but they have found it as hard to tell the good book from the bad as they have often found it to judge a man's real character before years of association have slowly brought some knowledge of it.

Our clergyman, as we have seen, solved this

ever present problem in a rough and ready way. Our ultra-æsthetic friends, the advocates of art for art's sake, solve the problem by practising the alleged trick of the ostrich, — they stick their heads in the sands of fallacy and say in their hearts, "There is no problem to solve." But what shall we do who want to order our conduct aright, and who want to read the books of the past and present that have won and are winning places in the literature of our race? I know of no simple answer to this question. I can say only that the more we read, the more we educate ourselves, the more we travel, the more we see of life, the more completely we realize that there is a diversity of tastes and opinions among men, the less the chance that the classic books of the past and the books of to-day vouched for by reputable authorities will do us any harm whatsoever. Experience seems to show that vile books and trivial books stand little chance of surviving. It also seems to show that every year added to our age diminishes the probability that a book containing questionable elements will do us harm either mentally or morally. But experience also shows that no critic or teacher can ever in this matter take the place of one's individual conscience. The book that by its descriptions of vicious characters and incidents merely amuses or interests one man in a harmless way may actually instruct another, and prove deleterious to a third. Any wide reader, if he is frank, will admit that there are certain books that he personally has never been able to read with profit — nay, even without loss. He will confess also that there are books which he can read in certain moods with enjoyment and no loss of self-respect, but which in other moods he cannot venture to take up. What is this but to say that we must all learn to read precisely as we learn to live — applying to the problem all the experience and all the conscientiousness we can. There is no royal road to learning or to reading or to conduct, nor shall we be helped on our way either by imitating our clerical friend or by laughing at him. He represents a class of pious souls we must reckon with — a somewhat decivilizing influence to be counteracted in legitimate ways. Time and education will give him and his like their euthanasia.

III

Actual book-burners are not so numerous as to set a dangerous example, but there are people who, in a sense, are determined foes to books — people who, having thrown themselves heart and soul into the philanthropical movements of our time, tend to prize literature almost solely as it makes or does not make for their own ideas of social progress, or, to be more exact, of socialistic propaganda.[1] Zealous spirits these, of true crusading quality — the stuff of which martyrs are made, — and if they did not exist, nay more, if they did not increase in our country, I should come as near as, I suppose, an American can to despairing of the Republic. Valuable citizens as these social enthusiasts are, however, I cannot but think that they go astray in their reasoning and lead others astray whenever they undertake to discuss the relations society sustains or should sustain to the literature and art of the present and the past.

The line of argument adopted by one of the most zealous social reformers I have ever known may be given almost in his own words. First, he thinks, with Tolstoy, that a man or woman should do his or her own share in the necessary

[1] It is interesting to compare their views with those of root-and-branch religious fanatics ; such, for example, as that Père Onorio whose extreme views on modern civilization are presented with great literary skill in Letter XI of George Sand's " Mademoiselle La Quintinie."

manual toil of the world, earning a living by the sweat of the brow, and not till then spend a moment's time in reading or writing or teaching or preaching, much less in ordinary money-getting. It is easy, to be sure, to offset this argument by the statement that the world has other necessary work to do besides the physical, and that it has discovered that by division of labor it gets all its kinds of work better done. It is not true, moreover, that only physical labor is accomplished in the literal sweat of one's brow. Brain workers suffer from exhaustion far more than hand workers, and if they were to earn their living as hand workers they would soon cease to be brain workers. This consequence would not disturb such social reformers as denounce, logically enough, art and letters and other high manifestations of civilization. But it must disturb those of us who have no preconceived theories — who are only striving to see our duty in this complex life and to do it. Yet, however much we may believe that this claim of the Tolstoyans that all men and women should do manual labor is erroneous, we ought not to shut our eyes to the fact that the Russian reformer has emphasized a great truth which most of us keep in the background. He has perceived that division of labor has separated men into classes which are alienated from one another through lack of sympathy caused by diversity of interests and disproportion of wealth. He feels that this lack of sympathy is the devil's work, not God's, for all men and women are children of God and should love one another according to the Golden Rule of Christ. He knows, furthermore, that to live in comparative luxury one's self while doing philanthropical work — whether giving money for charitable purposes or preaching or lecturing to the poor — is not the best way to assist our brothers, because it is generally done across a social chasm. So he has concluded that all of us who do not live by physical toil must cross the chasm and take up our lot with our brothers on the other side. My reforming friend thinks that this conclusion is correct, and has acted upon it. I think that the conclusion is wrong, but only in so far as relates to crossing the chasm. Let us try to fill it up instead — which brings us to the second reason of my friend.

A man's share in the world's goods, he says, is food to eat, clothes to protect him from the weather, and a roof to sleep under, for without these he cannot live. After he has these, he has

no right to anything more until at least this minimum is assured to all other men. When this is
done, he has a right to the same share of the
superfluity of this world's goods as another man,
the same right that his brother has through his
sonship to God. No man would be true to his
highest nature if he could be content to live in
purple while his brother by blood lived in rags;
but neither should he be content, while his brother
through Christ lives in rags.

Is this good reasoning? "It is rank socialism,"
some will say. Perhaps so, perhaps not; but the
main question is, Does this zealous reformer reason correctly, and does he lay down rules of action
that all should follow? For my own part, I think
that his reasoning requires only one emendation
to make it sound and obligatory upon all of us
who are trying to do our duty in this world.
Society has already assumed that every man has a
right to food, clothes, and a roof — a right which
involves, of course, the correlative duty to work
for them. Our organized charities and other
philanthropical enterprises may not secure this
right to all men in the best possible way, but
they really owe their existence to our acknowl-
edgment of this human right. Yet what of

the equal division of the superfluities of life?
Have we any right to more of them than our
brother has? This question will naturally suggest answers summed up in such words as " prop-
erty," " right of inheritance," " greater use of
opportunities," and the like; but I fancy that the
arguments involved in these and similar phrases
could be easily overthrown. I fancy that ethically
the contention that we have a right only to so
much wealth as every other man and woman has
is in need of but one qualification in order to be
sound. That qualification is, that we have a right
merely to such an extra amount of this world's
superfluities as will enable us to do to the best
advantage the necessary work of the world, especially that which is not physical. The physician
must have his instruments, the student his books,
the artist his studio and casts. But sheer luxury
for the sake of luxury, superfluous wealth to enable us to do little beside racing in automobiles or
playing golf, — no man or woman seems to have
an indefeasible moral right to, however clear the
legal or the prescriptive social right may be. And
here, again, the conscience of our age has begun
to make itself felt. The gifts of rich men for public purposes have their basis, not merely in indi-

vidual generosity and desire for notoriety or fame, but in a slowly growing perception of the great truth that no man has a right to any extra share of the world's wealth that is not needed by him for the accomplishment of the special work he is doing for the world. This may involve recreation, it may involve the appliances of art and culture, but it does not involve unproductive idleness, it does not involve the pampered existence of the votary of fashion.

How far wrong, then, was my friend when he declared that his conscience told him he was doing evil in accepting as his own more money than three families often have to live upon? After he had paid his board, he had sixty dollars a month left, and he did not know how to spend it in a way useful to all his fellows. So he gave up his salary for working with his brains, and went to working with his hands.

Was he quixotic? Perhaps so, perhaps not. He was wrong, 1 think, if by keeping that sixty dollars he could have bought books, educated himself still further, and, as an educated man, have accomplished more good for the world than he could possibly do by following the course he determined upon. He was right if, by sharing the life of the poor, he could become a better teacher to them and help to lift them up in the scale of civilization. Who is to decide this question if not the man who is most concerned?

But what conclusion are we reaching? From all I have said it would seem that I am in favor of letting each man decide how much he shall keep for himself of the wealth he is able to acquire. I believe that this is nearly the position we ought to take, provided we insist that each man make his decision with the most enlightened conscience that he can develop. The socialist on the one hand and the cynic on the other will declare that this is leaving the matter indefinite, and too much in the hands of very fallible mortals. But it is that and it is there already. My friend who has begun to do manual labor has had to choose his occupation, his clothes to wear, his food to eat, his room to sleep in. He has found it impossible to eschew superfluities entirely; he has had to choose what to do with five extra dollars a month instead of sixty. From the lowest estate to the highest this individual responsibility in the sight of God for our use of wealth and culture and time and labor must ever be felt, and, according as we answer to it faithfully, so will our lives be accounted worthy by

God and by our fellows. Neither the philosophy of complete renunciation taught by the mediæval ascetics and by Tolstoy, nor that of complete self-ishness taught by the hedonists of all ages, and especially by the gilded youth of our own day, can satisfy us. The problem is too complex for a simple solution. It will be solved, if at all, only by the enlightened conscience of humanity after the lapse of many generations. But I cannot help believing that it will be solved, not by all men getting on one side of the social chasm, but by all men striving to fill it up by throwing into it their wealth, their labor, and, if need be, their very souls and bodies.

Now to point the moral of this part of my discussion, which seems to be much more sociological than literary in character. My Tolstoyan friend and all who think like him are in a way infected with bibliophobia because they are jealous of the time and devotion able men and women give to literature and art, which seems to be subtracted from what might be given to the social regeneration of mankind. They belong to the not innumerous body of those who cannot make haste slowly. They see their high goal and dash impatiently toward it. They ignore the lessons of history and the complexity of life. They tend to forget the part that books and pictures and statues and music have played in developing the sympathies and rendering sensitive the consciences of men to the point at which philanthropy on a large scale has become possible. In their vision of an equalization of wealth they forget that, until the world has vastly increased its powers of production and its store of desirable objects, equalization of wealth would really mean equalization of poverty. They fail to realize how art and science, which minister directly and indirectly to increasing the efficiency of those directors of labor, those captains of industry without whom human effort, even under a co-operative or a socialistic system, would be in vain, so far as we can now see, — they fail to realize how art and science, which from this point of view have a strictly utilitarian value, would droop and die, deprived as they would inevitably be of the whole-hearted devotion of their votaries and, as the enthusiasts would like to have it, of their relations to the art and learning of the past. I say nothing of the loss of patronage they would sustain, because it is undoubtedly the intention of our socialist friends, when they come into their

kingdom, to substitute the social for the democratic public as the patron of the arts and
sciences. That much might be lost in any such
exchange of patrons seems possible, but the point
need not be dwelt upon.

What concerns us chiefly is the fact that it is
easy for the writer and the student of books,
watching the more ostensibly active and philanthropical work of others, to grow pessimistic and
to think of himself as "side tracked," as something of a drone. It is given to but few to
blend, like William Morris, the functions of an
"idle singer of an empty day" with those of a
socialistic agitator. Especially when one lives in
a large city and sees misery swarm but a stone's
throw from the haunts of fabulous opulence is
one impelled to close one's books and volunteer in
the war for civic and social betterment. There
is no reason why one should not, to a moderate
extent, yield to this laudable impulse; but if one
looks upon it as an injunction from heaven, one
is only too likely to close one's books in order to
follow a will-o'-the-wisp. To do thus is but to
show a distrust of literature and art as real,
though not so petty, as is shown by those
who distrust all art and learning that does not

advance the causes, religious and political, that they have espoused. In the last analysis your social enthusiast, your root-and-branch philanthropist, is as much a creature of prejudices as your religious or political partisan. He looks on to the future, while they, as a rule, look back at the past; he is an idealist, while they are formalists; but both he and they are far from being truly balanced, catholic-minded men, "looking before and after."

The real lover of books and pictures, the genuine student of letters and the arts, ought, on the other hand, to be of all men least the creature of prejudices and party passions and fanatical enthusiasms. It is his to enter upon and to enjoy the stored-up wisdom and the embodied beauty of the past, and he can do this without losing his sympathy with legitimate present efforts to improve the world or his faith in the future triumphs of the social spirit of man. He who loves books truly is by that fact enfranchised; he becomes a full citizen of the most ideal of all republics, the republic of thought and feeling. He who does not trust literature to do its noble part in the salvation of the race, who would shackle men's thoughts and kill their

books, the children of their brains and hearts
—even he who would persuade those chosen to
love books that their entire devotion is due to
more obvious and concrete forms of philanthropy
is careless or ignorant of his own best interests,
and is not to be listened to without danger by the
young and ardent soul.

VIII

THE LOVE OF POETRY

[A paper read before the Men's English Graduate Club of Columbia University, December 16, 1904.]

VIII

THE LOVE OF POETRY

THERE has been much discussion of late relative to the qualifications requisite to the successful teaching and studying of English, and, more particularly, of English literature. The topic I wish to say something about belongs, I think, among these qualifications, although it is not absolutely essential to good teaching or to fair attainments in certain portions of the field of English. It is a useful asset, rather than a *sine qua non*. If you will let me put it in Greek, now that I have already offended by deserting the vernacular, I will say that it is a κτῆμα εἰς ἀεί. The love of poetry — for that is what I want to talk about — deserves, if anything does, the encomium involved in the Greek phrase and in Keats's equivalent for it, " a joy forever." But I have known excellent teachers and students of English literature who were honest enough to lay no claim to this eternal possession.

Theirs was what we may call the sense for prose. Fiction, the essay, history and biography, criticism, prose comedy — in the interpretation of these admirable forms of literature they excelled. The poetic tragedy they could compass on its dramaturgical side. Society-verse, flying as it does at a low level, and some of the most characteristic work of Pope and Dryden, they felt to lie within their province. But for what some critics like to denominate essential poetry — for the masterpieces of Spenser and Milton, for the lyrics of Blake and Coleridge, for the subtle verse of Donne — for these and even for far less quintessential poetry, they would admit, in moments of confidence, that they had no genuine aptitude. On this side their teaching of English literature became perfunctory, and, like honest men, they eschewed it as far as they could. I wonder how many honest men and women there are to-day teaching prescribed English classics in our schools who would gladly leave instruction in the poetical texts to those of their fellows who are born lovers of poetry? I wonder how many of the girls and boys who must be drilled in those poetical texts would be glad to secede and to take up strictly prose work with those prose-loving teachers.

Let us suppose the exodus accomplished, and inquire into the probable results. Would the poetry-loving teachers, on the whole, do as well by their pupils as the prose-loving teachers? They might conceivably do better, if they were to give prose its due place in their teaching; for they would presumably teach poetry better, and lovers of poetry are not, in consequence of their predilection, necessarily insensible to the power and charm of the best prose. Poets themselves frequently write good prose, and a sense for prose diction and prose rhythms is, I think, for obvious reasons, to be expected of lovers of poetry. When poetry-loving teachers slight prose, the fact is generally due, not to inability to appreciate works of art composed in unmeasured rhythm, but rather to a yielding to the temptation to overemphasize the more cherished form of literature and to the perception of the greater adaptability of poetry to the purposes of the instructor, owing to its comparative succinctness. The teacher of poetry can deal with products that are artistic wholes complete in themselves more easily than the teacher of prose can; he can satisfactorily cover a larger number of writers through specimens; he can deal with the total work of more masters. Your prose writer bulks larger, as a rule, than your poet; and the matter of quantity thus making against the one, and that of quality, in popular estimation at least, making for the other, it would be rather strange if poetry-loving teachers did not somewhat sacrifice prose. I believe that investigation will show that they do sacrifice it.

If they do, and if prose-loving teachers tend to teach poetry perfunctorily, why should we not call matters even, except for those rather rare cases in which teachers who love poetry nevertheless manage to do ample justice to prose? Is there any good reason for ranking the teacher of poetry above the teacher of prose?

An affirmative answer is not, I fancy, so readily given to the latter question to-day as it would have been not many years ago. Poetry still holds, by force of tradition, its place of supremacy among the arts; prose still seems to many the product of a form of genius more pedestrian than that with which the poet is supposed to be endowed. But more and more we are being told that this is all an assumption. Lovers of music tell us that that is now considered, or else soon will be considered, the greatest of the arts. Some persons point to the growth of prose in scope and influence; to its flexibility, to its possession of rhythmic cadences, which to their ears are more satisfying than the cadences of poetry. They declare that ours is an age of prose, that the votaries of poetry, if more intense, form a smaller fraction of the total number of readers than was ever before the case. Against these assertions what has the lover of poetry to oppose except a personal conviction of the superior glory of poetry over all the other forms of art in which the human spirit has sought to express itself, or else the personal conviction of some other mortal or mortals, less fallible perhaps than himself, but still fallible? Will any amount of reasoning, especially of deductive reasoning, enable the partisan of poetry to put to silence the partisan of prose? I am inclined to answer in the negative. I see little use in arguing that the one form of expression is superior to the other, just as I see little use in denying that prose has caught up with or surpassed poetry in the estimation of the majority. When Matthew Arnold wrote that "the future of poetry is immense, because in poetry, where it is worthy of its high destinies, our race, as time goes on, will find an ever surer and surer stay," he may have proved himself to be an inspired prophet; but I am not sure of it now, although I could have sworn to his inspiration twenty years ago. Now, I blush to confess it, I am not even certain that I can analyze his sentence correctly. All I am sure of is that I hope he was right, provided I understand him.

But whither am I leading you? I began by announcing my purpose of talking about "The Love of Poetry," and I made a sort of separation of the sheep from the goats among teachers and students, and here I am basely surrendering poetry and one of her high priests, so far as lies in my power, into the hands of the Philistines. As a matter of fact, all that I have been guilty of so far is to grant that poetry may not mean so much in the future as it does to-day, and to express the opinion that it does not mean so much to-day as it meant in the past, if we may judge from the declining ratio of its lovers to the lovers of prose. This does not mean that I have felt my own allegiance to poetry abate one jot, or that I proclaim that allegiance without fervor and without the hope that long after I am dead and gone some one will be standing in my place proclaiming his allegiance to poetry in more effective tones than I can compass and to hearers even more keenly responsive than any of you. It merely means that in my judgment there are some causes that are served better through the witness borne by love than through the support rendered by argument, that I have very little confidence in the power of tradition to maintain for long any form of supremacy that has once been seriously questioned, and that finally, the older I grow, the less store I set by prophecy.

I return, therefore, to the proposition with which I started, a proposition which no mortal will deny, that a love of poetry is or may be made a valuable asset to teachers and students of literature, — a fact which may be gathered inferentially from a consideration of the value of a love of poetry to you and me as individuals.

But this is a theme that has occupied the pens of poets and critics ever since the Muses gave to Linus "to sing with a clear voice a song to men." Why not make a choice anthology of passages in praise of poetry, and read it, and have done? Chiefly because such a compilation is bound to be somewhat conventional and to lack the peculiar sort of appeal made by any one who bears personal witness to a conviction, a passion, an obsession. I propose instead to try to tell you

some of the reasons that make me love and value
poetry.

In order to get at the chief reason it seems to
me that I ought to ask what effect corresponds in
me with the inspiration which prompts the poet to
his highest utterance.   When the poet is in a fine
frenzy, to adapt Shakspere's phrase, what am I
in, or what should I be in?   I know of no better
answer to this question than that given by the word
— rapture.   A fine frenzy seizes the poet's heart
and brain, transmits itself to his verse, passes
through that medium into me, and, losing for the
time being its creative quality, is transformed into
that more or less passive state we call rapture.
This is to me the supreme value of great poetry,
that, more than anything else, with fewer draining
demands upon my store of vitality, my time, my
purse, — in short, upon the essential me and my
accessories, — it lifts me higher toward heaven,
opens my eyes more surely to the Beatific Vision,
wraps me " out of space, out of time," transmutes
me and transforms me more completely and
ecstatically than any other transmuting and trans-
forming agent of which I have knowledge.   I
readily grant that it is only the greatest poetry
which has this wonderful power, that there is much

poetry which gives me pleasure only, and often a pleasure differentiated but slightly from that given by prose. I grant also that rapture may be given by prose — for me personally chiefly by some of the prose of one poet, Milton, who, when he was composing it, slipped his singing robes half on, in a fit of aberration. But the main points are that great poetry more surely than anything else produces in me the most desirable condition known to me, — that of rapture, and that I can read poetry at all times and seasons and of all qualities and kinds, carried along by the hope that, if only by accident, the poet will fall into a fine frenzy and so cause me to fall into a fine rapture; or, if falling suggests dropping, and that in turn bathos, I will put it differently and say that I read on buoyed by the hope that the poet will soar aloft in a fine frenzy and carry me up with him into the heaven of rapture. For although I know by experience that I shall not often be carried all the way, I know also by experience that there are regions of delight short of the heaven of rapture, and spaces of quiet joy short of the regions of delight, and fleecy cloud-strata of pleasure short of the spaces of quiet joy to any one of which the capable poet may lift me, the confiding lover of poetry.

These metaphors which, without evincing conceit, I may call elevated, seem likely to mislead us unless we are careful not to draw inferences from them. It is correct enough to say that great poetry elevates, but it would be a mistake to suppose that great poetry is coextensive with what we call sublime poetry. The supreme English master of the sublime shows us in his so-called minor poems that elemental purity and rich beauty may make poetry great and induce in us rapture of the most authentic kind. The speeches of the Lady in "Comus," the flower passage in "Lycidas," the pictures in "L'Allegro" and "Il Penseroso," may produce rapture or something not far short of it, but they are not sublime poetry. I will admit that in my judgment rapture is rarely produced, as a rule, by anything that is destitute of the magical power of transporting us out of our present environment, indeed of carrying us far away from it. The poetry of commonplace sentiment, the poetry of modern realism, which is quite content to deal with steam engines and automobiles, and often succeeds in making them puff rhythmically, the poetry that bears the marks of any reigning fad or fashion, and hence never lets us forget that we are readers belonging to the first decade of the twentieth century — such poetry may frequently give us pleasure, and, when it is fresh, it may even give us delight; but I think it can give us rapture only when we are ignorant of the poetry which by transporting yields us, if I may play on words, true transports. This does not mean, of course, that the work of a contemporary poet cannot yield us rapture, for a great poet like Wordsworth or Coleridge can transport the few souls that first lend capable ears into new worlds of imagination and spiritual experience, and in those worlds those souls feel rapture unalloyed. All I would contend for is that poetry gains through age, as many pictures do, and that it is the transporting quality of poetry, especially of much of the best of the older poetry, that gives it, in conjunction with its universality, with its truth to life and to nature, the rapture-producing power with which we are dealing. Universality, truth to life and to nature, when they can be truly predicated of any work of contemporary art ought, indeed, involving as they must do the power of approximately perfect expression, to appeal to us profoundly and yield us rapture. Unfortunately, however, we are so constituted that there are a thousand chances that we shall see the universal in what time soon proves

to be but fragmentary and transient, to one that
we shall be able to recognize it in the rare work in
which it is really embodied.   Hence I think I am
right in advising you to seek rapture where it is
most certainly to be found — that is, in reading
the works of the great transporting poets of the
past.   It is great poetry — not the rapid transit
inventions of modern science, wonderful as these
are — that comes nearest in our mortal life to dis-
charging the functions of those admirable carpets
which in "The Arabian Nights" fly through the
air bearing hero and heroine to some far-off land
where the streams run felicity and the winds
breathe joy.

You will doubtless have perceived that I am
emulating the modern physicist who reduces
everything to a form of motion.   Rapture, — which
implies being snatched, — transporting, carrying
away — these are the words on which I have rung
the changes in this talk about "The Love of
Poetry."   But does not poetry give wings to the
soul, and are we not always wishing for wings?
Men wanted to fly before Dædalus, and they will
launch themselves for centuries from the roof of
the Smithsonian Institution.   The flying I am here
recommending is done much more easily and with

far less danger. And it is done not merely in
space, but in time. Borne upwards with Milton
we can penetrate the heaven of heavens; borne
backwards with Homer we can visit either the
ringing plains of windy Troy or the peaceful
homes of the blessed Phæacians, "mariners of
renown, outermost of men, living far apart in the
wash of the waves." We exclaim at the wonders
produced by the pressing of an electric button;
do they really surpass the wonders evoked by the
sight of a tiny group of letters —

"All the charm of all the Muses often flowering in a lonely
    word."

But some verbal stickler — are they ever real
word-lovers ? — may ask what I meant by saying
that I almost never get rapture from prose, when
I have just practically admitted that I can get
rapture from a single word. Do words lose their
qualities when a Milton turns them over to a
Burke? It would be foolish, I think, to answer
"Yes"; but while I stand convicted of verbal
contradiction and of apparent exaggeration, the
facts of my personal experience are about as I
have stated them. However much I may admire
prose, the stately march of Gibbon, the magnifi-

cence of Burke, the gorgeous splendor of Ruskin, the grace and ease of Arnold — it rarely or never induces in me the intimate delight, the gratitude, the reverence that accompany my reading of great poetry. Long experience has taught me this, and hence it is, perhaps, that I do not bring to my study and appreciation of the details of a prose composition a mind and soul so enraptured, so exhilarated as to invest them with a halo, a glamour. In studying, or better in enjoying, poetry, it seems to me that, partly through stored-up experiences of delight, partly through what I must vaguely call present flow and continuity of enjoyment, I am in a state of mind propitious to the discovery and appreciation of æsthetic beauties in word and phase and cadence — beauties which, as it were, accelerate the momentum of my imagination's flight or divert into gracious meanders my fancy's play. I admit that all I am saying is unphilosophical, unscientific, unworthy, possibly, of serious discussion. It may be only the illogical utterance of a misguided enthusiast who sees the arch of heaven in his mistress's eyebrow. But I have made no pretensions to being anything but a lover, and perhaps true love for poetry admits divided affections as little as true love for a woman does.

Perhaps the lovers of prose of whom I spoke, the honest men and women who confess they do not love poetry, are led by great prose to heights of rapture high enough to overlook those to which great poetry leads its votaries. Of that I know nothing and cannot know. I love great prose, I think truly, but I have adored — or, if that is too strong — I have given my allegiance to poetry ever since I was old enough to know that the prime law of our spiritual life is to give ourselves to something other than ourselves — to something better, truer, and more beautiful.

From illogical enthusiasm you will please permit me to pass to a sort of reminiscential garrulity. While I have remained true to my love of poetry ever since when, as a boy of ten or twelve, I used to declaim Byron's "Napoleon's Farewell" to a group of admiring relatives, — the relatives, I may say, admired me, but I admired Byron, and that admiration has withstood the stress and strain of thirty years, — while I have felt as though I should like to adapt the words of Coleridge and call upon the powers of nature to bear witness for me

> "With what deep worship I have still adored
> The spirit of divinest " Poetry —

I have had love affairs with quite as many different kinds of poetry as Cowley had with imaginary sweethearts. If I may trust the evidence of old books, — pathetically cheap editions, for modern poets were not to be found . in some Southern libraries at least, and a boy born in war times saw a dollar in the seventies about as often as your modern youth sees ten, — if I may trust the dates written in execrable copies of ecstatically prized volumes, it was Keats and his favorite Spenser that succeeded Byron in my catalogue of poet-masters; but it was Horace who first made me flatter myself that I might become a rational lover of poetry. This means that whatever critical capacity I have was first awakened by Horace — to whom I owe a debt and for whom I cherish a love which when I cease to acknowledge, deterred by modern undervaluation of his admirable poetic gifts, may my tongue cleave to the roof of my mouth. Shelley, Tennyson, and Pope followed almost immediately, and I was delighted by all three, and have no word of apology to offer for the combination. Then came Coleridge; then Longfellow, the only American poet I remember to have enjoyed in early years; for about my first acquaintance with Poe, to whom for one reason or another

I have since devoted many pages, I have absolutely no recollection. I recollect well, however,
that no alienation of South from North, no inherited belief that America had made but a poor
showing in creative literature, kept me from per-
ceiving, what I still in the face of over-subtle
recent criticism perceive, the essential worth and
homely charm of Longfellow's simple poetry. If
I had known Emerson and Poe then, I should
have thought, I am sure, as now, that it is the
great merit of the latter that he rarely or never
appeared in public without his singing robes about
him, and that it is the great error or misfortune of
the former that he too often knocked about in a
rhyming jacket.

How should I have thought otherwise then,
when from Coleridge I passed to Shakspere and
to Milton, and a little later to Sophocles? In
other words, could a youth of few books — but
those the best in English, Greek and Latin,
French and German — fail to perceive that true
poetry is as much a matter of style as of substance? How could I from the start yield
my full allegiance to any poet who does not
marry wisdom to immortal verse? As the years
have gone by, I hope that I have learned to

give to that line of Wordsworth's a flexible interpretation, — wisdom of a sort is married to immortal verse of a sort as well in Byron's " Don Juan " as in his " Childe Harold," most Anglo-Saxon critics in their native cant to the contrary notwithstanding, — but I trust that I have never for a moment ceased to believe that the Muse must be lovely as well as wise and good. This may be a digression, but I said that I would be garrulous, and I confess I am moved to as much wrath as is good for me, when I hear well-meaning people counsel other people to overlook a poet's technical defects and get at his message, in total oblivion of the fact that their favorite prophet or preacher is entitled to only a very low place on Parnassus. Many Browningites, Emersonians, Whitmanites, even Shaksperians, make me wonder whether, because sending messages with or without wires and with or without rapping-tables has become common, the chief end of existence is to receive them. Poor benighted Southerner that I was, I grew up in comparative ignorance of the latter-day cults of poet-prophets; the only message my poets brought me was that the gardens of the Hesperides need be counted no

myth, that I had but to open any of my well-
loved volumes to be transported thither, where
I could wander at will and pluck the golden
fruit. As I think of those unsophisticated days,
when I fondly deemed that poetry meant joy, —
not messages and ideas and problems, — I can
truly exclaim with Wordsworth, —

> " Bliss was it in that dawn to be alive,
> But to be young was very heaven."

And yet, poor heathen, there was no Emerson
or Whitman, or Walter Pater or Ibsen or
George Bernard Shaw or " R. L. S." or Rud-
yard Kipling for me. I had only the poets I
have named, — and some novelists like Thackeray, who was dead, and George Eliot and dear
old Trollope and excellent Charles Reade, who
were living, — and I added Moore and Campbell
and one or two other old-fashioned writers for
my acquaintance with whom, I suppose, if I
were not past forty, it would be my duty to
blush.

Some of the things I read were not designed,
I apprehend, for the perusal of a youngster. For
example, I took a rather thorough course in
Restoration comedy, and although the volumes

bore on their fly leaves the name of my grand-
mother, I do not care to shelter myself under
that respectable ægis. I am sure I should have
enjoyed Congreve, even if I had not known
that ladies read him a hundred years before.
I am equally sure that if I had had a father
alive who could have kept those and certain
other books out of my way until I was older,
I should have been no worse off. They did
not prevent me, however, from having as bad
a case of Wordsworth fever as any one ever
had on attaining his majority; nor did Wordsworth keep me from seeing in Homer, not
merely the Father but the King of Poets, to
whom I still maintain that Dante, Chaucer,
Shakspere, and Milton should make obeisance
as to their rightful lord. Yet Homer, Sophocles,
and Euripides, the writers I was reading
when people around me were praising the
men who were removing the reproach of literary sterility from the South, Sidney Lanier,
Cable, Harris, and the rest — even the great
Greeks, could not wean me from a love that
has grown with my growth and strengthened
with my strength — a love for those wits of
Queen Anne's day to whom Thackeray, who,

by the way, was never much attracted to great
poetry, so completely lost that capacious heart
of his. It was in the days following graduation
that I picked up at book auctions little copies
of Prior and Gay that I would not exchange
for their weight in gold. Cowper declared that
poor, ill-fated Robert Lloyd was

> " Sole heir and single
> Of dear Mat Prior's easy jingle ; "

but Prior was far more than a jingler, and he
left no heirs, only some very respectable collateral
relations. He and Gay can scarcely be described
as rapture producers, but the man they do not
charm has had some very humane elements omitted
from his composition. I felt this nearly twenty
years ago, and at a time when, strange as it may
appear, I was enjoying the work of Matthew Arnold and the treasures of Ward's " English Poets."
Nor could the glorious rhythms of Swinburne
or the deep, passionate poems of Browning, the
next objects of my adoration, make me swerve
in my affection for the eighteenth-century masters. I am certain — as certain as I am of my
existence — that a love of poetry is an unceasing
source of joy; I am almost equally certain that

a catholic, as opposed to a narrow, appreciation, is indispensable to any form of healthy love.

I have now given you "The Confessions of a Lover of Poetry down to his Twenty-fifth Year," which I hope are at least a little less naïve than some of the autobiographies more distinguished persons are persuaded to contribute to our magazines. I cut my recital short, not only because I do not wish to bore you, but also because I have carried it to the point where in addition to being a lover, I became a teacher of poetry. From being irresponsible I became responsible. Henceforth there was to be less flitting from flower to flower and more storing up of honey in a hive. I was soon to learn that the teaching and the study of poetry, as opposed to browsing in it, are attended by drawbacks that often try one's soul. It is not easy to talk about what one would rather worship silently; it is not easy to teach the delights of poetry to superior young persons who, with the wide knowledge of human life derived from afternoon teas or the football field, think of one as merely a harmless old fool; it is not easy to extend one's knowledge over the tremendous field of English literature in order that one may partly understand how the poets and the poetry one loves came to be what they are. Such of you as have taught already will know what I mean when I say that the teacher who has to feed gaping mouths —not ears — with choice morsels of poetry often wonders why schools and colleges exist. You will know what I mean when I say that the sight of rows upon rows of poets and commentators upon them that one has never read, that one scarcely hopes ever to get time to read, makes the teacher of poetry long for a better world where great verse will be diffused in the air, not gathered between the boards of books.

But while these difficulties of the teacher and the thorough student are very real ones, a love of poetry will enable him to surmount them as nothing else will. It is chiefly because this is so that I began by assuring you that the love of poetry is a possession forever. To poetry you can apply those marvellous verses of the youthful Poe to Helen — themselves an almost matchless illustration of essential poetic charm : —

> " . . . Thy beauty is to me
> Like those Nicæan barks of yore,
> That gently, o'er a perfumed sea,
> The weary, wayworn wanderer bore
> To his own native shore."

The spirit of poetry will not desert you when the day's work is over, and you are alone with your books. A line or two of a dearly loved poem, and you are under the spell and you will take up the task of preparing for to-morrow's class as though to-day's had not filled you with despair for yourself, your pupils, and some mighty poet in his undreamed of misery dead.

Yes, there is nothing like poetry for true restorative powers. Each of us, doubtless, has his own verse-specific which he not only employs, but takes pleasure in recommending. Mine are numerous sonnets of Shakspere and lines from the dramas, sundry periods of Milton, not a few whole poems and passages of Wordsworth, things of Byron, Coleridge, Shelley, Keats, Tennyson, and Browning — but more especially of Keats — yet why not say Palgrave's "Golden Treasury," with Ward's "English Poets" thrown in, and have done with it? How is one to narrow one's affections when English poetry resembles a field covered with daisies? And if one turns to other literatures, one experiences the same embarrassment. Some wiseacres tell us that the French have little genius for essential poetry, but many and many a time, reading this or that great poet in that exquisite

language, I have been tempted to apply to him
in my stammering way the words of Alfred de
Musset to Malibran, —

> " C'est cette voix du cœur qui seule au cœur arrive
> Que nul autre après toi ne nous rendra jamais."

And as for what the Greeks and especially
Homer have left us, and the tender Roman elegists,
— the smooth elegiac poets as Milton calls them, —
there is simply nothing to be said to those who
knowing do not love such inestimable treasures.
Men may be great philosophers and not love
Homer, — Herbert Spencer has just proved it, —
they may even appreciate many other forms of
verse and fail to come under his ineffable spell;
but if thirty years of devotion to poetry give me
the right to express a very positive opinion, I
will say that the man or woman who is denied the
privilege of undergoing the effects of Homer's
power and Homer's charm is deprived of a
rapture absolutely unique and supreme among
the raptures the Muses bestow upon their wor-
shippers. I know that this is mere assertion. I
can no more prove it than I can prove to a certain
friend of mine that a real Havana cigar is better
than the abominable weeds he genuinely enjoys

and regularly presents me when I dine with him.
There is no way known to me of proving that
Homer's Nausicaa is a creation of a higher order
than the astonishing heroines of some of our most
popular novelists; but fortunately the need of such
proof is by no means so great as the difficulty of
furnishing it.

The mention of Nausicaa brings, however, to my
mind what I can pronounce unhesitatingly to be
in my judgment the most consummate product of
the art of poetry that it has ever been my fortune to read. I am judging simply through the
quantity and the quality of the rapture it gave
me when I first read it nearly twenty years ago,
through the impression it has left ever since on
my memory, through the rapture it gives me to-
day. Nothing for me quite takes the place of the
pristine purity, the paradisiacal charm that ir-
radiates the sixth book of the Odyssey, with its
description of the white-armed daughter of King
Alcinous confronting on the shore of the sound-
ing sea, in all the dignity of maiden innocence,
the ship-wrecked favorite of Athene, the much-
wandered, much-enduring Odysseus. I have seen
great pictures that made the blood leave my
heart and rush to my cheeks and temples. One

such I specially remember — a marvellous, a divine
angel that burst upon me from a dark canvas by
Titian in a dark church in Venice. I have forgotten the name of the church and the subject of
the picture, but that angel and that moment of
unexpected rapture I can never forget. Yet even
this luminous point in my memory pales before
the moment when Nausicaa first swam within my
ken, when I first saw the thronèd Dawn awaken
her, saw her put on her fair robes and hasten
through the palace halls to tell her dream to her
parents, saw her standing tall beside her mother,
in the midst of the handmaidens spinning purple
yarn, saw her taking counsel with her kingly
father, saw her harness the mules to the polished
car, store it with the shining raiment, and take
her way with her maidens to the sea. As for the
game of ball played by her and her blameless
Phæacian attendants there in the dawn of time
beside the primitive waves, what words save those
of Homer are adequate to describe it! Who save
Homer could have put fitting speech into her
mouth before the naked stranger, or have filled
her mind with the innocent guile of the marriage-
able maiden? " Shakspere," you answer, and
thinking of Ferdinand and Miranda I pause—and,

after due deliberation, reply " Not so."   Beside
Nausicaa, even Miranda seems to me sophisticated,
though to say that appear at first blush to be
equivalent to saying that the sun in his meridian
splendor is jet black.   But I do say it, because it
was not Shakspere's fortune first of mortals to
behold the filleted Muses advance from out the
mists of the young world's dawn, and take their
predestined places upon their golden and eternal
thrones.